CONTENTS

Congregations. Change. Some days just to put those two words together seems like an audacious act of faith! Although God's desire for progress and growth is clear, somehow we often manage to clog the channels. Just how do we help congregations to change—to move toward greater health, greater mission involvement, greater passion for God and the divine agenda? Some days, I wonder. And then on other days—when I finally recognize that in this instance or that, congregational change has actually occurred— I am assured that there really is a God whose power is not just something our ancestors dimly remembered, but a living reality!

I have firsthand experience with the challenges of congregational change. I have served as a pastor for over a quarter of a century; 20 years at the Harbor Church on Block Island, Rhode Island, and the last six as an area minister for 50 American Baptist Churches in southeastern Massachusetts. I liken my ministry on Block Island to caring intensely for one plant. I weeded, pruned, watered, fertilized, and, occasionally even picked some fruit.

How I wish I had had a book such as this back in those confusing, early years. The tools available to me then were variations on a management-by-objective approach. Not a bad skill as one among others, but woefully inappropriate to the small, struggling congregation that through some quirk of providence had been entrusted to me. And yet by sheer dumb luck and some pluck, the congregation did change. We grew (from two- to five-dozen—and double that number in the summer!). We shifted from an inward to outward focus. We remembered who we were (the church in the center of town called to minister to the community), who are neighbors were (more than simply the year-round residents), and what our purpose was (to be the leaven of righteousness and love).

What I did not realize was that the process that worked could be replicated. I bumbled into a change process and did it only partially, but you have it available to you now in this roadmap, *Redeveloping the Congregation*, which melds the best of secular change theory (see John P. Kotter, *Leading Change*) with high quality theological thought and ecclesiastical experience. The result is a very usable map for leading change in a congregation.

There are many dimensions to the change process. Let us consider some.

Timing. Lasting change cannot be carried out overnight. I had a wise deacon on Block Island who counseled me, "Slow down, Tony. It takes as long to get out of a hole as it took to get into it!" I hope that is not literally true, but it is psychologically true. Patient, constant movement over the long term is more effective than a one-time big bang!

Culture. Every family or group or society develops patterns of behavior. These patterns allow it to function more efficiently, effectively, and smoothly. However, over time, these patterns take on a life of their own and become exceedingly hard to change. These patterns we call "culture." Culture has also been described as "the way we do things around here." These "patterns" or this "way" is the true target of our change efforts. New faces and new programs and new events and new activities are all good things. But if "the way we do things around here" does not also change, these new things will simply be like the sound of an engine revving while the congregation's transmission remains locked in park. Though it is difficult to effect cultural change, when the culture of a congregation changes, it can yield decades of positive results.

Tradition. Tradition is often understood to be the enemy of change. Although this can be the case, it is not necessarily so. Tradition is a powerful dynamic in our churches. Some people liken it to the anchor of the sailboat of congregational life. I prefer to think of tradition as the sailboat's keel. When the winds of change blow strongly, as they do in this period of history, a sailboat without a keel would simply capsize. The keel helps keep the boat steady as it uses the winds to move forward. Just so tradition can contribute positively to change.

I like the concept of self-adjusting traditions—traditions that invite congregations to examine key factors and adjust behaviors on that basis. The processes of examination can themselves become traditions. For example, an annual retreat in which congregational leaders gather to assess changes in the neighborhood that invite the church's response could develop into a tradition that helps the congregation continually change itself!

Energy. Change takes a lot of energy. One reason change is not normative in many churches is that it is simpler and less demanding to stay the same. Where then will energy come from to transform the congregation? It must come from the Spirit of the living God and be manifest through the passion of the people. Although it is good to have godly intentions, they are not enough. It is good to have high resolve, but it is not enough. It is good to rationally assess the purpose of the church, but that is not enough. The only lasting energy for change is spiritual energy. The Spirit must be at the center of our change efforts. As near as I can tell, it does not matter whether the congregation acts and is driven to prayer—or prays and is driven to action. But, for the sake of Christ, we must open ourselves to the power of God's Spirit!

Conflict. Where change is, there is conflict. Conflict is the collision of two or more ways or patterns fighting for the soul of one group! Conflict often takes a personal form. It can come from desire for control, fear of the unknown, willfulness, and the wish to stay in one's comfort zone.

Yet another motivation often leads to conflict: grief, mourning the passing (or the threat of the passing) of something that has been spiritually satisfying. Depression is a quiet way of living out this grief; conflict is a more active way. But grief is the underlying cause, and pastoral care is the loving response.

Related to this sense of mourning is the anxiety that results from feeling psychologically and spiritually off-balance. Imagine walking along and then stepping into a hole. The natural response is to flail about to regain one's balance. If someone is close to you at the moment of this flailing, then that one will most likely be whacked, slapped, or cuffed. Helping folk refine their balance is more productive than fighting this conflict on its presenting level. In this case, a hug is so much more productive than a reactionary shove!

Self-image. Finally, how a congregation sees itself has a huge impact on its change capacity. When church members see themselves only as victims of a hostile environment, they are likely to circle their wagons and resist change all the more. (After all, they believe, the change to date has not been beneficent.) Or they may simply despair of their capacity to conceive, implement, and sustain any significant change efforts. But a church that sees itself as an instrument of God, even if only in a limited way, will be free to act. And in taking even one step, this congregation can be empowered to continue the journey.

For the last six-plus years, my ministry has focused on a little garden, a group of about 50 "plants." When I survey this collection of congregations, I see that *change* is imperative. If we keep on doing things the way we have been doing them, we will keep on getting what we have been getting— smaller, weaker, disconnected congregations! Something has got to change if we are to be of any use for God's kingdom in the days ahead.

In this volume, the authors have addressed the major dimensions of this much-needed change. They have given us a theoretical understanding of the change process. They have admirably adapted Kotter's framework for congregations. They have provided us with a rich and detailed case study to enflesh the change theory. And, of greatest importance, they have provided a flexible yet amazingly detailed action plan for implementation of lasting congregational change efforts. If you seek to be open to the powerful, changing presence of the Holy Spirit of the living God, open this book nearly as often as you open your Bible!

ANTHONY PAPPAS

Declining membership. Decreasing energy. Separation from the community. Ministry that feels like "work." That is the land in which many churches live. Solutions abound. Assessment tools measure current reality and point to areas that must be addressed. A plethora of programs promise improvement in worship, newcomer assimilation, and small-group ministries, which will in turn save the church. Different companies offer demographic information about the neighborhood and community so efforts can be targeted. But in spite of following all the latest advice and excellent resources, many churches do not experience lasting change. The rush of energy these approaches bring quickly fades, and the church settles back to its original lethargy.

What makes it possible for a church to move from decline or stagnation into long-lasting vitality? How can a church immigrate from a congealing present into a compelling future? What can a congregation do to experience continuous, deep change rather than just temporary, surface improvement? How does a person lead redevelopment?

Looking for Answers

In 1994, after running up against those questions again and again, the three of us began searching for answers. As staff together at a church—lead pastor, associate pastor, and program staff—we wondered how we could best provide leadership to this church that we cared so deeply about. Within a year, life took us to different places. Gail retired and moved north, moving into church consulting work and becoming an active layperson in an aging church. Dan moved into an executive position with the denomination with responsibility for congregational development. Mary moved to a solo pastorate in a church experiencing serious decline, as well as working with other pastors and churches. Those questions increasingly engaged us. Our different settings provided us different perspectives.

So while our staff partnership ended, our regular discussions about congregational development and redevelopment did not. We intentionally made time on a regular basis to sit down with each other and share our experiences, our failures, and our learnings. Resources got swapped, books traded, and wisdom shared. The more we talked, the more curious we got. We engaged in informal research projects, searching for meaning in the experiences of other pastors and lay leaders, and reading everything we could get our hands on about change.

In addition to our other roles, each of us has related with dozens of churches as consultants. We have talked with and listened to hundreds of people who successfully and unsuccessfully have worked for and longed for their churches to be different. We found that programs and pastoral changes, by themselves, rarely made a significant difference. Successful redevelopment requires addressing the dynamics of change; it sounds so obvious as to not need saying. Yet over and over we saw promising change efforts ultimately fail, because the matter of change itself was not addressed.

Redevelopment Defined

So what do we mean by redevelopment? Our definition is simple. Redevelopment is the journey from life-threatening disease to life-giving vitality. Much like any living organism, a church has a life cycle.[1] A church begins life as a faith community with a passionate mission: to discover who they are, who their neighbor is, and why they are there. With all energy focused on those questions, soon the church possesses a strong sense of its gifts and strengths. It feels a clear call to a particular people or place. It knows its purpose. Energy and enthusiasm run high as the faith community starts to live that purpose out. Everything is new. Every step is a "first time." The energy supports innovation. Key to this part of the life cycle is the direction in which that energy flows. In a vital, healthy church, energy flows from God, through the congregation, and out to the people it is called to serve. We believe this inward direction (meaning it comes from God)

Figure 1: Life Cycle of a Congregation

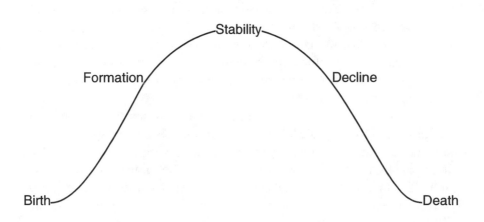

and outward focus (meaning it is directed towards others) is one of the most crucial and least tended to aspects of church health.

As a church matures, some of the energy naturally begins to be channeled inward to support emerging programs and provide an overall administrative structure. Those structures are as necessary to a church as a skeleton is to a human body. At this point in the life cycle a church must use some of its God-given energy for maintenance; however, the healthy mature church focuses only enough of its energy on maintenance to insure it can do its work well.

Often though, churches become preoccupied with maintaining and improving what they created. They hang on to the answers to the first and third of the foundational questions, "Who are we and why are we here?" but begin to neglect the second, "Who is our neighbor?" As long as the answer to that question does not change, there is no problem. But for most of our communities, that is not the case. They expand; they shrink. New population groups move in. The demographics of age shift. Every time the answer to "Who is our neighbor?" shifts, the equation formed by the three foundational questions shifts.

If a church does not notice that its neighborhood is changing and does not adapt its ministries in response to the change, the church will begin to decline. The sooner a congregation notices that disconnect and addresses it, the simpler the return to health. When the bulk of the congregation's focus is still outward, we think of the shift back as church renewal.

One measure of church vitality is adaptability. Can a church adapt its ministries to reflect changes in its own strengths or the needs of its community? Change is inevitable, so an inherent willingness to engage in ongoing renewal is a mark of vitality.

Revitalization is what the journey is called when the church's disconnect with the surrounding community increases and the energy has turned more towards maintenance and preservation. Revitalization requires more time and more energy than renewal.

Redevelopment is what the journey is called when the congregation has fundamentally congealed. The church now has become primarily focused on preserving the status quo. The congregation's God-given energy flows almost totally towards its own survival. When the faith community walls itself off from its community rather than living to serve it, death is inevitable. The only question is whether there will be life for that congregation on the other side of that death. The principles for renewal, revitalization, and redevelopment are the same. The congregation addresses change in all three cases. The greater the change, the more difficult it is.

Redevelopment: God's Call

Redevelopment is the resurrection journey. Like a bone marrow transplant or stem cell replacement, much of what seems intrinsic to the church will have to die. Redevelopment is an exodus. The congregation will have to leave many things behind to travel from captivity to the promised land. The journey is long. We have yet to see the immigration completed and the congregation settled into life in the land of ongoing adaptability in less than seven years. The cost is high. It takes everything a congregation has.

The result though is a faith community that is a living, breathing example of God's faithfulness and power. Its transformation becomes a powerful witness to others as well as to itself. New life really is possible. We are convinced that God has entrusted the church with a message. Life is stronger than death. Hope, more powerful than fear. Love makes all things possible. Redevelopment provides a faith community with the opportunity to personally experience that. Redevelopment is the call to be the Word made flesh.

The three of us are passionate about helping God's message be heard and experienced through the vehicle of congregations. We are convinced that dying and declining churches can experience resurrection. We have witnessed it and know it is possible. It does not come cheap though. It will mean letting go of some of the very things you and your church may hold most dear. Every yes will mean a no.

Redevelopment entails significant change, which is why the dynamics of change itself must be addressed. Assessment tools and programming helps will be important tools along the way. We do not downplay their importance and this book does not replace them. But they are not enough. Unless the dynamics of change are addressed, your church will slowly find its way back to where it was.

A Framework for Change

Our perspective is just that—our perspective. There are many. Some say that redevelopment is so difficult that rather than attempting it, churches should simply be allowed to die. When congregational resources, most importantly the will to engage in redevelopment, are minimal, this may be the best response. The landscape though is blanketed with churches in decline. These congregations want to be vehicles for God's activity in the world, but are lost at how to achieve that.

Other experts suggest that their way is the only way. We find value in almost all of them, and see the most successful redevelopment efforts using a combination. This book presents a particular framework for addressing change. It provides you with a particular set of lenses through which to look as you are addressing it. We interviewed pastors of successful and unsuccessful redevelopment efforts in our region. What seemed to make the difference was having an overarching framework to guide the journey.

Our framework for looking at the change process is provided by the work of John P. Kotter, a noted and recently retired (2001) professor of organizational behavior at Harvard Business School. His work on how change happens in an organization is heralded in the secular world as foundational to understanding leading change efforts. He researched change both in nonprofit organizations and for-profit companies. We have found that his findings regarding the process of change hold true for congregations as well.

Kotter's theory is that the process of change in any organization has a predictable and sequential landscape. He noticed that organizations embarking on the quest of change encounter eight key tasks along the way.

If the organization successfully addresses the task in front of them, they move a step closer to their desired goal. If they ignore it or address it inadequately, progress is blocked. The eight tasks or steps that Kotter identified are:

1. identifying a felt sense of urgency
2. establishing a coalition to support and guide the change process
3. creating a compelling vision of the future
4. clearly communicating that vision to the entire organization
5. empowering people to begin living out that vision
6. recognizing and celebrating the short-term wins along the long-term journey
7. dealing with systemic resistance (conflict) and barriers (ineffective structures)
8. anchoring the changes

Each task must be addressed in order. Developing a core team to guide the process precedes discerning a vision. When a step is successfully dealt with, it functions as a stepping-stone to the next one. When a step is ignored, it becomes a block or barrier that undermines the effort. Kotter found too that each succeeding step incorporates rather than replaces the ones that came before it. For example, a sense of urgency is needed not just at the beginning of the journey, but throughout. A guiding coalition or core team is necessary from the point of its creation onward. Both of those are essential tools in dealing with systemic resistance and barriers of step seven. A church that knows how to do all eight steps will be flexible and adaptive and can meet the challenge of any change.

Most surprising to us was that Kotter found that deep and lasting change was rarely accomplished in less than seven years. It simply takes that long for an organization of any kind to fully let go of old attitudes and patterns of behavior, and have the new ones permeate the system and anchor themselves. Redevelopment is truly the journey from captivity through the wilderness to the promised land. There is no short cut. No three-year version to opt for. Change takes time. How do you know when you are there? When the day comes that the church is inward directed and outward focused and the pastor and the lay leaders can be replaced without the system returning to where it was, then you know you have arrived.

That is the overarching framework for change that we are using. We also look at congregational redevelopment from a particular perspective.

These underlying assumptions frame how we view the change process and approach working with people and systems.

1. God is the one who brings change. God invites us to be cocreators and not only invites us but expects us to contribute. But, finally, God is the one who gives the fruit that we will bear.

2. Congregations and the people in them are fundamentally creative, resourceful, and whole. People really do know how to create God's beloved community. Leadership's challenge is to provide the time, space, and tools for congregations to discover their own answers.

3. Each and every person who walks through the door of a church is a gift from God. The gospel says each one brings with them gifts. The church's role is to help people find, develop, and use their gift for the good of God's creation.

4. How we are "being" with each other is as important as what we are doing. To do church effectively, means being church effectively.

5. Change in the church happens only to the extent that it happens in the lives of the people and particularly the leadership, both lay and clergy. Redevelopment is not something we plan with our heads and manipulate out there with our hands. Redevelopment involves our hearts—our total being. Our own lives are the embodiment of what happens in the systems we lead. A church cannot be transformed unless the people give themselves to transformation.

How to Use This Book

The eight chapters that follow address Kotter's eight tasks. Each chapter highlights a different one. Chapter 1 addresses urgency: the differing kinds and the one that a church needs, and how to develop it in your congregation. Chapter 2 guides you through the formation of a guiding coalition, a core team that will guide the change effort. Chapter 3 focuses on vision: making room for God's vision to be birthed in you. Chapter 4 guides you in helping the vision spread to capture the hearts and minds of the entire congregation.

Chapter 5 addresses empowering the congregation to live the vision that has taken root in them. Chapter 6 points you towards the fruits resulting from your work and the importance of honoring and celebrating them. Chapter 7 looks at the removal of any remaining barriers and the building of momentum. Chapter 8 addresses how to anchor the change so that the system remains flexible and adaptive.

Each chapter has three sections. The mentor section discusses principles and concepts. It provides theory and orients you to the specifics of what has to be addressed in each phase. The companion section takes you from the overview to the trenches, from the head to the heart. You begin to get a sense of what leading change is actually like for a person leading change in a congregation. You move beyond the theory and begin to taste the emotional content of the experience. While stories are very real, Valley View Church is not. It is a composite.

The coach section provides specific ways for you to begin and stay focused on the work of redevelopment. The intent is not to guide you step by step through a redevelopment process. The intent instead is to help you develop the unique processes that will be effective for you and your church.

First, read through the whole book to get a sense of what this seven-plus-year journey will be like. If you are a pastor, share it with your leadership team. If you are a layperson, share it with your pastor and others in the church. Everyone providing core leadership needs a sense of the general nature of the journey they are embarking on. It is helpful to have an overall understanding about the process—where you are now and what is coming next.

Go back then and focus on where you currently are. Each chapter gives you a sense of the work to be done for that part of the journey and how to assess when it is time to move on to the next stage of the journey. The coaching section asks you to journal in response to certain questions. We suggest you journal throughout the process of redevelopment. The journey is rich and your own insights will be invaluable. God will be present and active throughout. Journaling will help you stay aware of God's movement. Later, your journal entries will be an "ebenezer,"[2] reminding you of those points in the journey where you saw God act.

Our definition of a good theory is "one that lasts long enough to get you to a better one."[3] May this theory of Kotter's adapted for the church setting serve you well. All of us are always learning. We would love to hear from you as your journey unfolds. Your experiences will be invaluable to those that come after you. Share too with others around you. God is active and alive in our world, bringing hope to the hopeless and life to the dying every day. Each time people share the good news they have witnessed or experienced, another person or another congregation finds the courage it needs to step forward into the life that is waiting for it.

Blessings,

MARY, DAN, AND GAIL

NOTES

1. For more information on the life cycle of a church see Alice Mann, *Can Our Church Live? Redeveloping Congregations in Decline*. (Bethesda, Md.: The Alban Institute, 1999), 1–12.

2. Still found in hymns today, *ebenezer* is an old word that comes from a Hebrew word meaning "stone of help." When ancient people on a journey encountered the Holy in a real and felt way, they constructed a pile of stones to mark the spot where God had acted. This ebenezer was a sign to all who passed, that God had been experienced there.

3. Ken Wilber, *A Theory of Everything* (Boston: Shambhala, 2000), xiii.

1

Surfacing and Nurturing A Sense of Urgency

Observations from a Mentor

So, you are considering embarking on the journey of redevelopment. This may not be your first time. Perhaps you have started the journey before and experienced your efforts getting you nowhere. Such past experience may leave you skeptical about beginning again; and yet, deep within, the desire remains. You long for your church to live into the potential you know it possesses. That desire urges you to try it one more time. You want your church to become what God has in mind for it. That is exactly what it takes to begin.

World-renowned change expert John Kotter is clear that developing a sense of urgency is the first step towards lasting change. The journey of redevelopment leads a church and its leaders through discouraging valleys and over steep and challenging mountains. Turning back or simply stopping along the way constantly tempts you. Only commitment grounded and fueled by a sense of urgency will sustain you for the long haul.

The journey is long. Though the details of the journey differ from church to church, there are eight tasks or steps that are common to all. Desire to reach the destination quickly lures you to ignore or only superficially address those tasks. New programs that offer the promise of quick growth entice you. But your goal is not just an improvement of the present. Resuscitating your church is not enough. It needs to develop the ability to remain flexible and adaptive in a changing, shifting environment. Nothing less is the goal. But without a compelling sense of urgency, perseverance fades. The journey is once again abandoned.

Urgency as a Response to Crisis

Urgency comes in many different forms. Some forms effectively motivate and energize groups to achieve short-term results. Crisis can serve a good purpose, spurring people to action. The shout of "crisis," much like the cry "fire," draws an immediate response. Volunteers to teach Sunday school fail to step forward. Declining worship attendance leaves the sanctuary uncomfortably empty. Income falls short of expenses. All these things create a sense of urgency born of crisis.

Any crisis initiates a rush of adrenalin. Urgency in the form of a threatening problem to be solved brings quick action. Once solved though, people relax and the urgency fades. The urgency of crisis draws action that restores stability. The deep systemic change of redevelopment requires a different kind of urgency. The redevelopment journey calls for an urgency that motivates and sustains the long-term commitment needed for deep change.

Urgency Born of Opportunity

Urgency can also come as an opportunity calling for immediate response. A crisis, or a problem, provides an urgent call for restoring the system to a familiar place. A new opportunity invites the church into something new and different. An influx of immigrants in the neighborhood presents an opportunity. An immediate caring, supportive welcome draws them to the church. The opportunity is greatest before they settle into community patterns that do not include the church.

A disruptive or tragic event in the community provides a short-term window of opportunity for the church to engage a segment of the population in new ways. An unexpected call from the school principal offers the opportunity to become a partner in an after-school program for children.

Both urgency of crisis and urgency of opportunity compel a church to react. After responding though, the church easily moves into a satisfied resting place. Successful crisis management rewards the church with a feeling of security. A met opportunity may result in the improvement and enhancement of the church's ministry. Both are satisfying. However, though they initially bring great energy to the surface, in both cases the urgency disappears after a successful response. Nothing deep or foundational shifts.

The goal of redevelopment is to shift how a church interacts with its emerging environment.[1] The long journey of redevelopment requires a more compelling and sustaining urgency than either opportunity or crisis can provide.

A Holy Urgency

A midsize church had indicated they were ready to add a full-time associate pastor. They wanted to grow 50 percent in worship attendance and knew they would need additional staff to accommodate that kind of growth. As a support person from the denomination, I began to work with the church as they began the process of adding a staff person. We met one Tuesday night. I started the meeting with a simple question, "Why do you want to grow?" People said: "With more people, we can have a better quality youth group." "All of our programs can be strengthened and expanded." "Our choir will be bigger." "The building will feel better on Sunday morning with more people in it." The focus of their answers was *inward*, on making the church a better place for them. They wanted more of the good things they were already experiencing.

One woman listened and expressed a different view: "I am concerned about those people who live in the very nice houses in our community. They are prosperous people, but their lives are desperate and empty. I am also concerned about the ones living near poverty level, who are losing hope. They all need what we in the name of Christ can offer them." She voiced an *outward* focus.

The lone voice also communicated an urgency. She talked about what would make the difference between life and death for people. She expressed her sense of God's call to the church. The call was grounded in God's own urgency, God's deep concern for the well being of all of God's children. Her voice expressed a holy urgency.

The meeting that evening lasted two hours. They looked at worship attendance records of 20 other churches of similar size and of the same denomination in that part of the country, attendance records spanning 30 years. They saw how attendance for most of the churches had not changed more than an incremental amount up or down, even ones where staff had been added. At the end of the evening the committee was clear that adding staff was perhaps something for the future, but not the present. The committee began to sense that without a widespread ownership of a holy urgency, nothing would change in the church. They decided to dedicate the next meeting to exploring together the passions that were within themselves, the urgency they felt as they reflected on more effectively presenting the gospel to seeking, hurting people in their community.

God authors the only urgency adequate for church redevelopment. The urgency from God focuses on God's mission for the church. The focus is outward on people in need of the life-giving gospel. Only an urgency born of God provides the energy and sustenance for redevelopment.

An Urgency of Life and Death

For deep and foundational change to happen in the church, only an urgency of life and death suffices. Unlike urgency born of crisis, the focus is not on the life or death of the institution. This urgency is about the lives of people. Urgency permeates the life of a church as it understands the life-giving nature of the gospel entrusted to it. An outward focus on the needs and hurts of people, flowing from an inner awareness of the power of the gospel, sustains the church for the redevelopment journey.

One person put it succinctly as she told why she gave herself in ministry through the church. She reflected on her life and her home situation during her teenage years. Raised in an abusive family environment, she told how the church and the gospel had made the difference between life and death for her. Persons in the church were a real, living, present Christ for her. Their caring sustained her and developed her self-esteem. The church and the gospel released her from a hell of self-judgment and hopelessness and opened the door to life. In response, she did everything she could to be the life-giving presence of Christ for others. A driving urgency to be Christ for others guided her life long after any crisis was solved or opportunity embraced.

Only the awareness that your church can and will make the difference between life and death for people provides the urgency for redevelopment. Without that outward focus on the well being of others, a sufficiently compelling sense of urgency will not be present. You may start the journey with good intentions, but the costs outweigh personal gain. Only shifting from desiring benefits for yourself to being compelled by the benefits for others provides the motivation.

Developing an Outward-Focused Holy Urgency

Churches regularly pray for others in general ways. One leadership team regularly, in a disciplined way, lifts individuals for prayer each time they meet. Their prayer though is different. They pray for persons whose lives are not presently touched by the church and the gospel. They mention specifically what they sense to be the desperation, hurt, pain, and hopelessness of these persons. Trusting God to work in God's own way and time, they envision specific ways they sense the church could connect with these people. Their regular, vivid prayers help keep alive the outward-focused, holy urgency in their church.

Discomfort and fear often stop people from reaching out and connecting with those they do not know. Reluctance increases when people differ ethnically, economically, and physically. A person in a wheelchair unable to talk may provide a social challenge for some, as might a recent immigrant with limited English. For many of our churches, the persons in the neighborhoods do differ from persons in the church. Setting aside concern for personal comfort and focusing on the well being of others can be a strange and scary place. Holy urgency is urgency about the well being of others: it motivates people to face and move beyond their fears in order to walk beside and with others who differ.

People face doors every day that block their way into living a life of joy and fulfillment, doors that hold them back from becoming fully what God created them to be. The awareness and conviction that the church really does hold those keys to unlock doors will provide the motivation, the staying power for the journey. Only the powerful sense that the church can make the difference between life and death provides the urgency that sustains people on the journey.

Personal Experience Is the Basis

Personal experiences provide the source of holy urgency in the church. The strength and depth of the individual experiences of the life-giving power of the gospel provide the foundation. Remembering what God has done in their lives, people become aware of what God can do in the lives of others. People need to develop their own "ebenezers"[2]: those markers, symbols, and rituals that remind them of the past and present life-giving presence and action of God. Only that awareness keeps alive the urgency and provides the motivation and staying power for the journey. Churches do not have a sense of holy urgency without the people in them having a sense of holy urgency.

At first, perhaps only one person in a group may be able to articulate an urgency to reach out to people in need of a life-giving faith. How does a group move from that one person to all the people feeling a holy urgency? Start with the simple awareness that most of the people in a group and most of the people in the church have personally experienced the life-giving power of the gospel. In one way or another, the gospel and the church have made the difference between life and death for them. Their stories may be deeply buried under layers of social norms that work against telling those stories. For some people the doors unlocked so gradually that they have no key conversion moment to point to. Factors work against both an awareness of and an atmosphere for telling the stories. But those stories of the difference that the church and the gospel have made exist deep within people.

One church prided itself on being liberal and middle class. Theology was debated but stories of faith experiences were shunned. A workshop helped leaders identify their spiritual journeys and the peak life experiences that had shifted and shaped their lives. People began to talk about those peak experiences as transformational moments and they began to see the transformational moments as times when God had been quietly present in their lives. With encouragement, before long these formerly reticent people were sharing their stories of the life-giving acts of God in worship settings.

Nothing needs to be done to create a sense of urgency. First, simply invite people once again to get in touch with what is already deep within them. Nurture a culture that not only permits, but invites telling the stories. The sustaining, empowering holy urgency essential for the redevelopment journey emerges only as the circle of awareness widens. In time, the remembering and telling moves from a small leadership group to increasing numbers in the church.

Create a place of comfort for reflecting on personal values, for remembering personal life stories. Provide safety for people to begin to talk with others about those stories. Create places of comfort and safety through careful listening, honoring the uniqueness of each story. People are ready to talk about what the church and their faith mean to them. They just need the permission to talk, someone to model how to talk, and someone to listen.

An Emerging Sense of Urgency for the Church

How does a sense of urgency emerge in the church? With permission and modeling, some people begin to talk in gentle and low-key ways about their faith journeys. As committees go about their work, they begin to raise questions about what really is important in life and in the church. Others begin to wonder out loud what is important to God and where God might be attempting to lead their church. Something new begins to be formed: a new sense of values, a new sense of the mission of the church. People remember their own movement from death to life. With the awareness and encouragement of others, they become aware also that God entrusted the life-giving gospel message to the church. The purpose of church grows clearer, and passion about its mission blossoms.

Remember that this is only the beginning of a process. A clear vision of the redeveloped church of the future will emerge later. A clear vision developed and presented too early shuts out the creativity of others and limits ownership. Avoid the temptation to talk about a clear vision, a specific picture of the future for the church. Trust God to give the vision when the time is right.

Developing awareness of the deep longings within hearts forms the solid base for moving on into transforming the church. Without the conviction that what the church offers makes the difference between life and death for a person, redevelopment is not for a church. The church that now exists may be improved. Growth may happen. But people will not have the will or the staying power to move into something significantly new.

To allow that solid base of urgency to emerge takes time. How long? Certainly months and maybe a couple of years. It begins by individuals reflecting on their own lives, how God has been present and active for them. Begin that reflecting. Become aware of the difference the gospel makes for you. Your companion will let you know what that journey was like for her and your coach will help guide you for this part of your journey.

Reflections of a Companion

If you are facing redevelopment, I have stood in a place similar to where you now stand. I wonder what you are feeling at this moment. Excitement? Fear? Trepidation? Skepticism that it is even possible? Eagerness? Take a moment to name the word that best describes your feeling.

Do not ignore the feeling. Be with it. Place your hand on the part of your body where you feel that emotion most strongly. Take a few slow, deep breaths and simply feel it. Strong emotions are part and parcel of the redevelopment process. Right at the start, learn to notice them. They will bring you invaluable clues about what is going on in and around you. I find my own emotional and physical responses to be an invaluable barometer. My hand starts rubbing the back of my stiffening neck long before my mind realizes I am feeling uncomfortable. At a thousand points during the redevelopment process, knowing that I was angry or fearful allowed me to deal with the anger and the fear as something resident in me. No one made me feel those things. The arduous journey of redevelopment brought me face to face with my own demons.

I cannot predict what the redevelopment journey will be like for you, but I will share what the journey was like for me—perhaps that will be helpful. I have never been more challenged, more energized, or more despairing. I have never felt more supported and more alone.

To educate and prepare myself, I read books, attended workshops, and talked to clergy and laity. All helped. But when things got rough, and they did, only my inner sense of God's call, my own personal sense of holy urgency, kept me going. When seemingly insurmountable blocks to the process arose, I found myself turning to my own faith story. Remembering past experiences of God's activity and faithfulness in my life anchored and calmed me in a way that nothing else did.

A Personal Experience of God

I had gone to church as a young child and then drifted away. It was not until my mid-twenties that I started attending again. I deeply appreciated the fellowship I found there. But oddly, I found an anger within me that I had not known existed. It bloomed when I saw power being misused and people being oppressed by the very institution that claimed to be about freeing them. I would be sitting in worship, fuming about the latest occurrence, when the anger would transform into hope. I would find myself dreaming about a church where each person was honored, where each gift was valued—a church that truly lived as the body of Christ.

A cross-country move led my family to a new church that embodied the very way of being I had imagined. It was a community of committed Christians who were internally motivated and externally focused. Grounded in God and extended in love, their doing flowed from their being.

There, I experienced what it was like to be viewed as a beloved child of God who had been given unique gifts for a unique purpose. The church was like a playground or a laboratory. We could explore our gifts and test them out in the safety of a loving and supportive community before venturing further afield with them. I had been a shy child with stuttering speech, but they helped me discover and claim a gift for speaking and for leadership. The church provided me with places "in-house" to take risks and develop new skills. They supported me when it was time to try out those skills in arenas beyond the local church. I felt like a butterfly emerging from my cocoon. As I started to fly, I loved nothing better than watching and helping others do the same.

God's Call

With my two children soon to be in school full time, I started thinking about what was next for me. I had loved staying home with the boys, but now other things beckoned. One summer Sunday morning after worship I poured myself a mug of coffee and wandered into Sunday school. I sat down next to Lori who had just graduated from college. "So what's next?" I asked. She told me. What came out of her mouth astounded me. It was exactly what had been running through my mind of late.

She explained that she was most likely going to apply for a master's degree program in English, and teach. "You don't sound real excited," I commented with a sideways glance. After a long pause, she added, "I guess I'm not. What I really want to do is go to seminary. That's where my heart is; my passion. But I don't know. It's not right to just choose to be a pastor because it's what I love and where I feel alive unless God calls me."

"Lori," I heard myself saying, "Have you ever considered that your love for it, your passion, *is* God's call to you?" With those words I knew that I was talking to myself as well as Lori. I began seminary studies that fall . . . on the 35-year plan. But as often happens, once the goal was identified events conspired to remove the barriers. I finished in four years.

Eight years following that day back in Sunday school, I sat at the closing worship service for an annual conference, the yearly denominational meeting of pastors and laity. I was an ordained minister being considered for appointment to Valley View Church, a troubled congregation in a troubled community. From the moment I had heard about the opening three months before, something within me said I would be the one to go there. There was no doubt in my mind though, that with my lack of experience I was the least likely to be chosen.

The bishop was preaching that morning from the Gospel of John. "Peter do you love me? Feed my sheep." Tears streamed down my face as a glimpse of the future filled my head. I suddenly knew three things: I was going to Valley View; it was going to grow to be a place of hope and healing, a powerful conduit of God's Spirit; and both the church and I would pay an enormous price for it. It would take everything we had.

A New Beginning

The phone call came the next day along with the question if I would consider coming. The church's staffing committee, our denominational support person, and I all met together for the very first time on a warm and breezy July evening. We chatted, each trying to determine if this would be a good match. The people were pleasant and friendly and yet there seemed a certain guardedness about them. I could not put my finger on it, but I had a hunch something was not being said.

Near the end of the evening I asked, "If I were a stranger who moved in next door to you, what would you tell me about your church?" There was a long silence. All I could hear was the wind against the house. Finally one of the women shifted uncomfortably in her seat and said slowly, "I wouldn't tell you anything. I wouldn't want to inflict our pain on you." The others nodded.

Their hurt and shame was palpable. I could feel it. And in the months that followed, that encounter was played out over and over again. Late one afternoon a middle-aged man stopped by my office. He stepped inside and closed the door. "I want you to level with me," he said. "Are we dying? Have they sent you here to close us down?"

Valley View had been doing vital ministry for over 100 years. But 10 years of watching attendance, giving, and energy decline had them believing they had little left to offer anyone in the way of good news. The most they hoped for was an easing of their own pain and the church's survival.

And even their survival was now in question. Financial constraints were felt in every area. Even more troubling to them, this church that had once been known in the community for its children's and youth ministries, now had only a tiny handful of each. It was clear to them they could not continue on this path and survive. A sense of quiet desperation pervaded the church. They no longer saw themselves as a church with problems, but as a problem church.

It's All in Your Perspective

Although the challenges were evident, I felt confident. The indicators for redevelopment were all there. They still had critical mass in terms of worship numbers. Their location and facility were excellent. More important than any of those factors, I was totally convinced that God had plans for this place. I did not know how it would happen, or when, or even what the church would look like when it was all said and done. I simply knew that the time had come for God to transform and work through this church in powerful ways.

While the people's perspective about themselves was fairly negative, I chose a more positive one. The people were gifted, compassionate, insightful, and had a heart for God. In their daily work and volunteering in the community, these people made a real difference in the life of real people every day. They helped the children of migrant farmworkers learn to read, taught school, provided services that allowed the elderly to stay in their homes, worked at food banks, and supported cultural diversity. The more I came to know them, the more I appreciated them and found myself thinking, "I cannot wait to see this unfold!" My sense of urgency built: "These are people who have been gifted with exactly what this valley needs—compassion for the marginalized and a desire to make a difference"

They had lost the ability to see themselves in that light. Although people might want to come hear me preach, they did not see that they as a church had much to offer anyone. They did not see how by linking their gifts and their placements in the community, God could work to heal a city that was torn by racism, classism, and poverty. In the midst of their pain and fear, they had lost touch with their past experiences of God working in and through them. No longer living and experiencing the truth of God's promises of hope and wholeness, their evangelistic urgency had congealed.

An Urgency of Crisis

They did, however, feel an urgency to fix their problems. Participation, finances, and energy neared a critical point. If that were not enough, a winter of heavy snow had left us dependent on more than a dozen buckets to catch the water dripping through the ceiling. There were concrete problems that could no longer be ignored and people felt an urgency to address them. And I was the one, they believed, who could fix their problems.

Because of family considerations, six months separated the sealing and announcement of my coming and my arrival. It was not unusual in those months to receive phone calls and even visits from people at the church wanting direction. What were my recommendations about changing the worship services? How should they run confirmation? And what about . . . ?

We decided that it would be best if we waited until I arrived in January. What I heard in them was a sense of urgency. Things needed to be addressed and they needed to be addressed *now*. Life had become uncomfortable enough that they were ready to make changes and were open to trying things; things they might have rejected if everything had been going smoothly.

That was exactly what I was looking for: an urgency that would help them start moving. It was not the kind of urgency that would serve us well long term, but it would at least get us going. A former pastor of mine once told me that you cannot steer a sailboat that is standing still; you get it moving first and then work on the direction. The simple truth of that had stuck with me for years. The church did not feel the kind of urgency I would have chosen for them and it would not sustain them for long, but perhaps their sense of impending doom would at least start them moving.

Egypt had once been a land of milk and honey for the starving Israelites. Only when it became a place of unbearable captivity and oppression did they find the motivation to leave. That seemed to describe us well. The people did not seem to care where I led them, as long as we moved away from the place of death and despair.

Their dependence on my leadership gave me great freedom to try new things, but it felt terribly uncomfortable. I am most comfortable with a style of leadership that coaches others. I had to continually remind myself that my goal was to provide effective leadership in this setting, which required me to give people the kind of leadership they needed, rather than the kind I most liked to give. Sometimes that meant being more directive than I am naturally comfortable with. The key learning for me was the importance of staying focused on what they needed rather than what I needed.

Struggling with the Role of Leader

In that first year, I struggled with my role as leader. People looked at times to me as they would to a firefighter during a fire, imploring with their panicked eyes, "Just tell us what to do." Much of the time I did not know what to do and the dependency I saw in their eyes frightened me. They trusted me to lead them from captivity to the promised land. Not only did I not have the map, but I remembered all too well from the Exodus story how quickly people could turn on the leader once the initial crisis was over.

The experts who I read and consulted with and who I trusted the most, advised me to rely on God and my intuition: to trust that if I loved the people and made myself available to the wisdom of God on their behalf, all would be well. The words of Julian of Norwich, 12-century Christian and mystic, became my mantra, "All shall be well, and all shall be well, and all manner of thing shall be well." The people thought I was reassuring them; really, I was reassuring myself.

On the other hand, I felt a tremendous freedom to experiment. Not only did I believe in God and in the people, my denomination believed in me. They provided strong and encouraging support. They partnered with me and with the church. All three of us—people, pastor, denomination—were clear from the start that the plan was redevelopment. What a tremendous difference it makes when someone believes in you. With that kind of support behind me and the vision God had planted in my heart before me, I was filled with a holy urgency about my task.

A New Kind of Urgency

The urgency that Valley View needed to feel was not the stressful kind that results from a crisis; nor was it the excited urgency triggered by a once-in-a-lifetime opportunity. We needed to feel an urgency that was strong, deep, and unstoppable, like a mighty river of life flowing through us into the community. This was an urgency that would bring the real hope of a higher standard of living to the migrant families and working poor of the community; an urgency that would build bridges of understanding between groups experiencing serious disconnection: Anglos, Hispanics, and Native Americans; growers and farm workers; young and old; gay and straight. Ultimately, this was an urgency that could create a community marked by justice, compassion, and love.

Our focus would be outward, but our motivation and direction needed to come from within, from a deep and personal sense of God's call to us. So even while we tended to the urgent "fix-it" things, we began to cultivate the deeper urgency. Under the leadership of the previous pastor, the church had begun to get more comfortable with talking about the spiritual life. If they were to continue to grow in that ability, I would have to support it. It was a stretch to learn to talk openly about my faith story, my God experiences, and my call. But when I was able to share my story even in simple ways, others seemed freed to share theirs too. What a gift it was to hear other people's God experiences. It reminded us all just how real and faithful God is.

So whether you be clergy or laity, what has been your experience of God? When have you felt God nudging or calling you? What is your sense of God's will for you as an individual and for the church you are a part of? The answers to those questions are the best resources you have as you prepare to lead redevelopment. Blessings as you explore them with the coach.

Guidance from a Coach

Welcome to the first coaching section on the journey of redevelopment in your local church. As your coach, I am excited to join you on this journey, even though our relationship is through this one-way medium of printed word. Whether you are a pastor or a layperson initiating this process of redevelopment, you will find the following steps helpful. Additionally, it will be beneficial to begin keeping a journal of your reflections throughout this redevelopment process. At a number of points along the way, I will urge you to record specific items in your journal.

Surfacing a sense of holy urgency is the first consideration in the process of transformation and redevelopment. To do so, one must first begin by focusing on individuals. The deep inner longings that God has planted in each person will become the foundation for discovering the collective sense of holy urgency in your particular faith community. As individuals share about their faith experiences, their places of deep passion, their encounters with God, their agonizing sorrows, their glimpses of the "kin-dom" of God, their places of willing sacrifice—their reflections will point to the collective sense of urgency God has for your congregation.

Reflect and Journal

Let us begin by clarifying what you will accomplish in this coaching section. The goal for this session is for you to identify and explore your own sense of holy urgency, and to develop a plan for surfacing the sense of holy urgency in individuals in your church. Be aware that this section, like the other coaching sections that follow, will take many months or even years for you to complete. Be patient; let this section take as long as it takes.

As you begin to explore your own personal sense of holy urgency, consider the following questions:

- When did you first have an awareness of God's presence in your life?

- Who were the early witnesses of God's love for you? In what ways?

- Describe your call from God. Include those moments when you knew you were claimed as a child of God, and that God has a vision for your life.

- Is there a particular biblical story or passage that you especially identify with? In what way?

- What do you find yourself being very passionate about?

- What do you find yourself being willing to sacrifice for?

- Is there a particular setting or situation in which you frequently encounter God? How do you listen for God's leading?

- What has God been saying to you most recently?

- Are there other questions or areas that you would like to be asked about?

Find the time and space to reflect on these questions. Record your response to each one as clearly and completely as possible in your journal. This will help you to surface your own sense of God's holy urgency within you. As you reflect on your responses, which ones did you expect to hear from yourself? Which ones surprise you? Why? How might God be speaking to you through these surprises? How does this help to inform you about your own personal sense of holy urgency?

Develop a Plan

Review the following plan for surfacing the sense of holy urgency among individuals in your church.

- Prepare to have individual conversations with persons that mirror the reflections above that you just responded to.

- What are the settings in which you might have these individual conversations with persons? Do some of these settings already exist? Do they need to be created?

- During the next month identify three or four persons with whom you will schedule these intentional individual conversations, make the contact, extend the invitation to talk together, and get each conversation scheduled.

- At the end of the first month, evaluate the process you used, refine the questions you ask, and then repeat this process on a monthly basis for up to a year, talking with three or four individuals every month.

- Remember to always keep the questions individually focused and not on the corporate church. At this point you want to learn about their personal journeys of transformation, not their vision for the church.

- Consider the spontaneous moments in other settings that present themselves, when God is nudging you that now is the moment to ask a question or two about one's faith journey. Challenge yourself to watch for these moments. Be listening for when things are revealed about someone's sense of holy urgency at meetings, informal gatherings, coffee hour, and so forth.

- Record in your journal what you are sensing from people. Rather than attempting to record exactly what people have said at the time, record your impressions immediately after your conversations, allowing you to truly focus on the persons sharing during the conversations.

- Note additional options to learn about the inner sense of holy urgency in various individuals.

Chart a Course

Now it is time for you to commit to a plan of action. Review the suggested plan listed above. What steps will you take to move forward in surfacing the various expressions of the sense of holy urgency that God is stirring up within your church? Write down as clearly as you can the steps you will take and the time frame for each. For example, who is the first person you will have a conversation with, when, and in what setting? By when will you extend the invitation? What questions will you ask this person? (See the initial reflection questions you journaled on for ideas.) Remember that this is an unfolding process that may take a year or more to discern.

Is God nudging you that this is the time to get started? If so, begin now. If not, take the time to reflect on what God is calling you to do at this time.

Looking Ahead

As you discover more and more about the sense of holy urgency that God has planted in the people of your church, you may also begin to sense a need to involve others in this process. That sense will lead you to the next step you need to consider in a redevelopment process: forming a core team.

NOTES

　　1. Interaction with an emerging environment is a recurring theme for a church in redevelopment. Robert Quinn, Change the World (San Francisco: Jossey-Bass Publishers, 2000) 78–79, presents the concept of the importance of this interaction. This theme is found throughout Quinn's book.

　　2. See note 2 in the preface to this book.

Forming a Core Team

Observations from a Mentor

After talking with people for a number of months, you will begin to feel the beginnings of that holy urgency we talked about in the previous chapter. Open yourself to people, and in response, they will begin to open themselves to you. You will come to know others who share with you an outwardly focused sense of urgency.

Who will be your companions in this early stage of the redevelopment journey? Ultimately, the goal is for everyone in the church to be companions. But to reach that goal, a small group of enthusiastic but patient people must first form. This group can have a variety of names. Some call it a guiding coalition. Others call it a core group. We will call it a core team.

Members of a core team open themselves to each other and to God through prayer, study, reflection, and dialogue. They share a sense that God is calling your church into something new and different. They search for what God has in mind for the church.

The Challenge of Patience

Some things demand direct and immediate action. An especially toxic person who is abusive or someone who creates a legal liability requires response today. Building repairs may demand attention right now. Programs and ministries that nurture the growth of members need to be continued and improved. Opportunities arise requiring a response.

The normal operations of the church are addressed by individuals who step forward and by elected committees. But redevelopment, the transformation of a church, is different from maintenance and improvement of programs. Redevelopment cannot be accomplished overnight. Nor can it be carried out by an individual or an individual with a few enthusiastic friends. The challenge even exceeds the ability of existing committees.

As people begin to get a sense of what might be possible for their church, they want to move into a significantly new place quickly. Eagerness is good; however, patience in redevelopment is essential. An energetic, enthusiastic pastor may find one or two laypeople who share the enthusiasm and want to charge forward yesterday, not tomorrow. Or an enthusiastic layperson, sometimes someone new to the church with a new vision, feels an internally compelling mission. And, for that person, today is the right day for bringing in sweeping changes. But the core team looks beyond the immediate needs. It moves away from quick results.

The Core Team: A Formative Microcosm

The formation of the core team and how that team works together significantly influences the outcome of the redevelopment process. The core team will be a microcosm of the church that will emerge, the yeast that will slowly permeate the whole system. The membership of the core team and the values they embody as they work together molds the church of the future. What is created now, how it is created, and how it works together exerts a powerful, formative influence.

Laity and clergy giving initial leadership in the redevelopment process have some inkling of an embryonic vision. This initial glimpse of where God is leading may shift dramatically in the process of emerging, but it provides in this moment initial direction about who should be included in the core team.

Who should be part of this core team? Accomplishing a shift in the church requires broadening the leadership. Current leadership exerts a significant formative influence on the current state of the church. In addition to including some current leaders, also include people who are not currently part of the leadership. Who these people are depends on the church's situation and early hunches about the vision. If your sense is that the geographical neighborhood is your focus, the core team eventually must include people who are neighbors.

Your church may interpret who your "neighbor" is more broadly. You may feel the beginnings of a call to connect with a particular group, perhaps a generational group or persons with a specific lifestyle or life situation. In that case, the core team would include representatives of those groups.

During the early stages of formation, the core team's task is spiritual formation and the development of community. As it pays attention to its own internal life, however, maintaining an outward focus is a challenging priority. Offering the keys to life to people beyond the church remains foundational. Without the holy urgency of this goal, the redevelopment journey flounders.

Importance of Diversity in the Core Team

The more diversity embodied in the core team, the greater the ability to respond to the diversity of the neighborhood. What does the community look like now and what are the projections? The ethnic makeup, economic and educational levels, and other lifestyle differences are key. If God calls the church to focus on the geographical community, the core team must reflect that community.

Leadership for redevelopment also requires diversity of talents and strengths. Some members of the team are strong in strategic thinking. Some members have talents in responding to and using conflict in appropriate and creative ways; other members are excellent in articulating the core values and vision. Some members are action oriented and others are stronger in empathy and compassion. No individual person has all the strengths needed to lead an organization in a major task. Through interaction in the team, individuals discover new talents, and new strengths develop. The multiple strengths essential for leading on the redevelopment journey are present in the diversity of the members of the team.[1]

Strategic thinkers, persons strong in empathy, futuristic visionaries, persons able to see how parts are connected, others who see and develop potential in others—an effective core team needs them all and more. On the redevelopment journey, add new persons who bring what the team needs for each part of the journey. Developing a dynamic, changing organization requires a dynamic, changing leadership team.

The church needs ongoing, stable groups. Buildings, budgets, and personnel require that you follow tested and established procedures. That is not true for the core team, which will shift and flex. The makeup of the team today only foreshadows the makeup tomorrow. The team vigilantly seeks to discover the new diversity offered by God. For the sake of more fully becoming the future church God has in mind, the microcosm is always open to change.

How the team relates and works together is important. They embody a foretaste of what they are creating. The future church will mirror the way members of the core team relate to each other. For example, do they value honoring each other? Do they see each other as creative, resourceful, and whole? Do they function in a truly collegial way? How do they ground their life in scripture and prayer? Do they reveal joys and pains to each other? How a diverse core team relates today shapes how the church as a whole will relate in the future.

A Continued Life-and-Death Focus

Members of the core team explore how the gospel is a life-and-death issue for their own lives. The core team of a small church separated from their urban neighborhood invited a newer attendee to join them. Janet lived down the street from the church and was a 26-year-old single mother with little previous experience in church. Her faith had been awakened through her participation with the Alcoholics Anonymous group that met at the church. Over the past year, Janet had begun attending worship services and the weekly Bible study. The saving and transforming power of God was very real to Janet. Her experience helped others on the core team remember their own transformative faith experiences. Past and present experiences fueled their urgency to make the life-changing, life-giving gospel available to others.

The common thread of personal faith experiences is what holds a diverse team together. And, their experiences of personal transformation better prepare them to lead the transformation of an organization. They understand from personal experience the cost of new life—they know it is worth the price. Leaders of redevelopment need skills, knowledge, and talent. But nothing substitutes for experiencing personal transformation in equipping people as change agents. Only individuals who experience deep personal change can lead the process of deep organizational change.[2]

A powerful past experience of deep change, however, is not enough. The goal is to create a system, a church that will continually adapt and shift in a shifting environment. To create a church capable of continual redevelopment, leadership must come from persons who have committed themselves to continual, ongoing transformation in their own lives. Motivated by a past act of God in her life, a leader can bring a single major shift in the ministry of a church. But what is needed in redevelopment is the ability to shift in an ongoing way. Persons who experience ongoing shifts in their own lives are best equipped to lead in a continually changing environment. They have developed the ability to let go of what they have relied on for security. They are confident that what is life giving for the future will emerge.

How a Core Team Is Formed

Different churches form core teams in different ways. Many times it begins with the pastor simply looking for others who share something of the same sense of holy urgency that she does. Out of informal conversations she begins to explore common passions. Individuals begin to mention others who they feel would bring valuable gifts and perspectives into the conversation. They share a common concern for people, for the spiritual and physical well being and the wholeness of people. And, they have experienced and are experiencing God at work in their lives. Together through prayer, study, reflection, and dialogue they attempt to discern what God has in mind for their church.

In other churches, the governing board of the church may be asked to select or endorse the creation of a core team and clarify the initial assignment given to it. God has many diverse ways of working. A variety of approaches can achieve the same results if key leadership remains clear about the purpose of this part of the redevelopment process.

Dangers in Forming a Core Team

Two dangers in the forming of a core team are disconnection from the church and leadership that now exists, and being so connected that the vision and redevelopment process is constrained. If the core team simply reflects the norms, patterns, and vision of the present constituency, the best that can be expected is improvement, not transformation. On the other hand, if the core team is disconnected from the church as it exists today, valuable resources for redevelopment are lost.

The pastor in one church heard the verbal affirmation given by long-time members to redevelopment. He also sensed their tremendous resistance to change as new and different people were being brought into the church. Excluding long-time members totally from participation in the core team was the way he chose to deal with the resistance. Having no voice, they experienced disempowerment and alienation and over a three-year period left the church. During that time, persons newer to the faith and from a lower economic level were brought into the church; however, the maturity and financial resources of the long-time members were gone and the redevelopment journey suffered. Ultimately, the newcomers did not stay either.

How do you keep connected to the healthy and much needed resources that are already available while opening the system up to the newness that God wants to bring in? That is the challenge both in determining the makeup of the core team and in choosing the process for forming the team.

Include several people from among the current leadership as core team members. Consider people who are able to envision and lead into the future. Valuable human, as well as financial, resources are already present in the church, even those churches experiencing the most drastic decline. These resources are crucial in a redevelopment process.

Representative members of the groups that will also be invited into the emerging church need to be invited into the core team. These are not necessarily persons who have rushed forward to volunteer as leaders in change; rather, they are persons who are eager to live as part of a community. They give themselves to discover with others what God has in mind for the future. They join with others to experience and embody the new life into which God is calling the church. With their presence, the church that had been encased in a shell learns to interact with the broader community.

An Official or Unofficial Group?

But should the core team be an official group of the church or informal and unofficial? Although it may initially emerge as an unofficial group, most churches find that at some point recognition needs to be given to the group. For the sake of the redevelopment process, however, the core team continually has to be shifting in its makeup. Only by shifting and reaching for ever-greater diversity and inclusiveness will the redeveloping church avoid encasement in simply a new and updated shell. The church needs to authorize the core team to guide the church in the redevelopment process. The core team must be free to lead in real change rather than simply improving or maintaining what currently exists.

Conflict can emerge throughout the redevelopment process—it sometimes appears very unexpectedly. The process of forming the core team is often a place where early signs of conflict can be experienced. People begin to sense that something new is emerging. They welcome a hope for a better future for their church, but they expect that better future to happen without any personal cost. Early in the process some may begin to feel that their position and leadership are threatened. Questions are asked about what "that" group is doing. "Don't we as the established, officially elected council have the responsibility and authority to provide leadership and make decisions?" Balancing a concern for honoring faithful, elected leadership with a concern for the emerging health of the entire church is not an easy task.

The Task of a Core Team

A key question for a church is: "What does a core team do?" The function of a core team is to ensure that the church stays on the redevelopment journey; the objective is to maintain movement. How the core team does its work varies: in one church the team actually engages in planning and implementing processes and activities for each part of the journey, and in another church, the team is a more invisible, behind-the-scenes group. The team is an informal but significant network of persons, and these persons provide creative leadership in significant places.

In one church the elected administrative council, several years into the redevelopment process, began to function in ways similar to the initial core team. The council centered itself more and more in prayer and scripture. It began more intentionally to look at the overall health and direction of the church. Response to the broader community and vitality became the focus rather than simply hearing reports from existing groups; however, a core team did remain. As a body not responsible for maintenance, it could focus more on the new ways God was leading. Both the core team and the council remained attentive to where the church was on the redevelopment journey.

How long does it take for the core team to form? It depends. In one situation, it may happen as quickly as twelve months; in another, it may take three years. But the formation of the group is essential before individuals rush to the next step. Your companion will let you know about her own experiences during the forming of her core team. Your experience will be unique, reflecting who you are and your ministry situation. But her experience can give you a sense of what to expect.

Reflections of a Companion

Before coming to Valley View Church, I had been rather a lone ranger in my leadership style. I enjoyed and worked well as a member of a team. But when it came to providing the overall leadership, I did not like sharing it. Sometimes I did not trust the people to care as much as I did. Sometimes I did not trust myself and did not want others to know that. Mostly though, I do not think I trusted God enough to let go of control. This next phase of our journey of change challenged me in all of those areas. The time had come for me to learn how to trust.

I had read John Kotter's work prior to my arrival at Valley View Church. His first step of establishing a sense of urgency made sense to me. Urgency provides motivation for change. Of course. His second step, gathering a powerful group of people who together would provide the leadership for change, made just as much sense. I imagined a group of well-respected people who felt a holy urgency towards a common goal. Change would be inevitable, I thought.

Good-bye Control

But while I embraced Kotter's first step towards change, I feared this second one. It felt so uncomfortable. Did anyone else feel the kind of holy urgency I did? How could I find out? And if I found these people and gathered them together in a room, what would we do? What if they disagreed with me? Or thought me foolish? Then what would I do? The real question was did I think that redeveloping the church was all up to me. If it was, then fine; I could hang on to the control. But if I believed that God was bringing the change not through me, but through us, well then, there needed to be an "us" for God to work through.

Substantial change in an organization, said Kotter, required more than any one leader could provide. I believed that. I believed too in the priesthood of all believers—that all are gifted and called to be conduits of God's wisdom and love. I decided a core team would be the best approach, and the faithful approach. Not knowing how to form a core team, I talked to other pastors who had done it successfully. Each, I found, did it differently.

One pastor met weekly with all the elected committee chairs and team leaders. Another pastor gathered people informally, twice a month on Saturday mornings for coffee and bagels and discussion about the church. A third pastor personally invited 12 people to participate in a book study on congregational change. Some core teams met in highly structured ways, while others had a looser dynamic. Each seemed right for its setting and circumstance. None sounded quite right for us.

This was the first of the scary lessons. No one could tell me which was the right way for us. No formula existed to tell me who precisely should be part of the core team or what we should do when we were together. Valley View and I needed to figure it out for ourselves. That figuring out took time, and the first hurdle was deciding whom to gather.

Gathering the Group

I used four criteria in gathering the initial group. I had heard church consultant Roy Oswald once say that a church could grow no deeper spiritually than the people at its core. I knew I wanted spiritually alive and growing people on this team. That was the first criteria.

Second, the team members needed to be powerful. Wise and soft-spoken, Elena held no official role in the church, and she had never chaired a committee in her life. But when Elena spoke, the older women listened and nodded. If Elena said that something was so, her wide circle of friends believed it. This team would be charting a course into unknown and potentially unsafe waters. Not only did we need the best wisdom available, we needed it to be spoken by voices that inspired trust.

The third criterion was diversity. Because the team members would be providing leadership for the entire church, they needed to represent its breadth. Where Elena had the ear of the older women, Robert connected particularly with those folks under 55. When church members looked at the core team, I wanted them to be able to see someone who looked like them, someone who had once faced similar concerns. We also needed people in that group who represented the people not yet in our church: young adults and non-Anglos.

The fourth criterion was attitude. The members of the core team had to be willing to work together and trust each other. Elena and Robert were givens, but who else? Puzzled, I finally gathered the three of us together, laid out the idea of a core team, discussed the criteria, and asked them who else they thought should be on it. They quickly surfaced three more people; we invited them, and the group lurched into being. The church council had blessed my gathering an informal group to reflect on redevelopment, but we had no official role in the church. We had no formal power as a group, no tasks charged to us, and no decisions to make. Our role was to watch, learn, reflect, and share—a think tank of sorts.

Discovering Its Task

Our times together were awkward for many months. We knew how to run committee meetings or accomplish a task, but no concrete task existed for us. We chatted, we dreamt, we got to know each other, and we prayed, but mostly what we did was carve out some space for God. Freed from the responsibilities of doing, we were free to focus on simply being. Deadlines did not push us, nor did business consume us. In the beginning, our job was to sit around and drink coffee and enjoy each other and wait for God to show up. It was as if together the six of us formed a womb for the new thing God was birthing in our church.

It took time to grow comfortable with such passive work. I remember one evening, perhaps the fourth or fifth time we had met. We had gotten past the "hello, how-are-you's" and were discussing a quote and some questions I had brought. About 40 minutes into it I found myself wondering what television shows were on that night. Looking around at the others, it appeared as if I was not alone. "Is this boring?" I ventured. Truly nice people, they hemmed and hawed. "Because," I confessed, "I'm bored. I'm feeling like this isn't working very well tonight." "Root canals are better," someone finally groaned. Everybody laughed and the dam opened. We spent the next hour in energized conversation around what would make our times together compelling for us.

It took us a long time to find what worked. I am the one who made it the most difficult. Once we had identified the people, I quickly formulated a vision of our core team: what we would do, how often we would meet, what it would be like, and how we together would provide leadership for the change effort. Things were starting to develop so fast, I could almost taste it.

The only problem was the structure: what worked perfectly for me was not what worked for many of the others. They had other preferences and brought with them their own visions. Finally, we all laid aside what we each knew would work, and experimented. Different people came up with different ideas for us to try.

One Wednesday evening the core team sat in Ira's living room and watched the movie *Norma Rae*. A journal at his workplace had recommended it as a movie that dealt with leadership and change. Afterwards, we ate ice cream and discussed the nature of leadership.

Elena ushered us into her kitchen early one Saturday morning and put us to work making bread. We learned firsthand about the importance of not rushing a process, and how one basic dough can yield vastly different loaves.

We talked about teamwork as we helped Joe move into a new apartment. In addition to chatting about church and change, we talked about God. We shared our God experiences and tried different prayer forms and spiritual disciplines. Some of the things we tried worked well for us; others flopped. Always, we ended with a time of gentle critique. What did we want more of? What did we want less of? What did we want to stay the same? Our goal was to find ways of being together that assisted us in experiencing God in our midst and that encouraged our discussion of the overall movement of Valley View along the path of redevelopment.

I remained the official leader of the core team, but my leadership style changed. I began to see my task as creating safe and sacred space where team members could exercise their own gifts of leadership and wisdom. Ira and I were often the ones who found articles and books for the group, while Elena often led the discussions on them.

Changing with the Times

What evolved across time was flexible and organic, and the shape and nature of our core team shifted from year to year. The first year we met, the six of us came together about every three weeks. The second year, we invited the committee chairs and team leaders to join us. As a bigger group, we met less often and used a more formal structure when we did. The third year, our core team took yet a different shape. The church council and the core team came together to form a larger joint leadership team. At that point the leadership of the core team shifted to be shared between myself and the chair of the church council. Looking back, each form was right for its time.

But to this day, I still feel some level of shame about all the shifts in form our core team experienced. On vulnerable days, my gremlin gives me a hard time about it saying, "If you really were a good leader, you would have built a core team that looked like what a core team is supposed to look like." Despite what he says and despite how I feel in those moments, I know that what we did worked for us. We built what worked for us, and we built it together.

The critical thing was always having a core group of some kind that was acting as yeast, dreaming about the future, looking frankly at the present, and searching for God within and without. So while the form varied, the function stayed the same—looking at where we were and where God was in the midst of that and what God was doing.

As time went by, the people in the core team began to see beyond the urgency of the day-to-day crises of the church. Their hopes and dreams for the church deepened. Their hunger for change sharpened. They began to taste the possibilities, and as they did, their circle of friends and acquaintances in the church did too. They truly functioned as yeast—their energy and commitment leavened the church.

Who Really Brings the Change?

In those core team meetings I came to really know that it was God who would bring change to the church and not me. It truly was not about what I wanted or what the church or the denomination wanted. God meant to do something here and we could either be in God's way or on it. I found myself shaped by those gatherings. I could be vulnerable there in ways I was not in other groups, sharing hopes and dreams for my life as well as for the church. We ministered to each other.

The core team gave me a great place to check things out. "It seems to me that folks are hanging around longer after worship. What's that about?" "We seem to have a number of folks with allergies and asthma. What would you think about an 'unscented' Sunday once a month?" "What do

you suppose are the implications of the School Levy failure for the church?"
As a group, we did not have responsibility for making decisions about those
things, so it had more of the feeling of a sandbox or a playground: freer and
more creative.

And when conflict arose, the core team was invaluable. From the very
beginning we had examined a number of different change theories. All
suggested that conflict was an expected part of the creative process. So
when it finally showed up, we were not surprised. For some, conflict
confirmed that we were on the right path and the church really was
experiencing change. Having reflected on the church on a regular basis,
we could see the big picture and knew the right questions to ask. We were
able to stay calm and focused in the midst of conflict and be a nonanxious
presence. God was at work.

Because of the time we had spent praying, turning to God in those
difficult moments was natural. The nature of our time together had given
all of us an experience of how a healthy Christian community behaves. I
believe that is what made all the difference when we faced difficulties. It
was not just me. A group of us stood together and responded calmly,
thoughtfully, prayerfully, and sought what was best for the community of
the church and the community we were called to serve. Others noticed and
followed suit.

The Gift of a Team

It is hard to find the words to express just what that meant to me in those
times. Support, encouragement—yes. More than that, I knew I was not
alone. I might hold the role of pastor, but I was part of a team. We were in
it together. That helped me focus fully on the issues being raised rather
than putting energy into protecting or defending myself.

Funny to think back on how I resisted forming a core team. How
frightening giving up control seemed. Having been through it now, I cannot
imagine doing it without them. Even if it were possible, I would have missed
so much. There is something to be said for going to the places that scare
you.

How about you? What do you think about a pastor and a group of laity
partnering to lead change? What would be the challenges in your setting?
How might you begin? Blessings as you work now with the coach to
determine exactly that.

Guidance from a Coach

The next step in the redevelopment process is to form a core team. The mentor and companion have helped you consider the need to gather together a group to guide the continuing work of redevelopment in the church. As a coach and church consultant, I have frequently witnessed the insight and power that is generated when a group of people comes together in intentional ways for reflection. This often requires setting aside longer or more frequent periods of time than is typical in conducting church business. This set-aside time provides the space in which to hear and discern God's intent.

Reflect and Journal

The goal for this coaching section is for you to develop a plan for forming a core team to guide the process of redevelopment in your church. Having just read this goal, note how you are feeling about the prospect of forming and working with a group like this. Are certain blocks coming to your mind in attempting to form such a group? Make a few notes in your journal about your thoughts and feelings at this moment.

In preparing to form a core team, it will be helpful to envision what such a group might look like and do. God has already planted the vision for this team in you. Use the guided meditation provided on the following page to help you describe this future core team, which in turn will help you identify possible people to serve on such a group. Ask someone else to read the next portion to you when you are ready to fully engage in it, so that you can close your eyes and be taken where God wishes to lead you.

Guided Meditation

Settle into a comfortable position. Allow your eyes to close, and begin to focus on your breathing. Breathe in and out slowly and deeply. With each breath you become more and more relaxed. You are sinking into a very quiet and calm place. This place leaves the noise and stress of the outside world behind. Distractions fade further and further away. It is a place of peace. You begin to sense God's presence there. It feels like a place of acceptance and love.

You gradually become aware that others are present. You notice the comfortable surroundings that all of you are in. There are about 10 people at this gathering. Like you, they all have a sense of the holy urgency God is calling them to. You are drawn to this particular group of people. You feel a deep sincerity in their welcome.

Consider the atmosphere of this gathering. What is the setting like? How are the participants interacting with each other? What does it feel like for you to be with them? Is there a discussion taking place? If so, note the topic. What other activity is taking place? How are you engaged in the activity of the group?

Simply be present with this group for a while. What are the prevailing attitudes people are exhibiting? What kind of energy seems to be created here?

The group is preparing to conclude its time together. Notice how they draw their time to a close. Participate with them in their closing, and prepare to leave them. As you depart, you have a sense of being refreshed and relaxed. As you gradually return to this room, sit quietly and remember the group with which you have just been. Breathe in the remembrances. As you are ready, open your eyes.

Take a few minutes to write down everything you can remember about your experience with this group. Note the details of the setting, behaviors, the very essence of the group, and your reactions and feelings. What drew you to this group? Now go back and note any ways that this informs you about the nature of the persons you may wish to consider in forming a core team.

Develop a Plan

Now let us look at a suggested plan for identifying a core team in your church.

- Consider which persons you encountered in your conversations about holy urgency for whom you had an affinity. Refer to the journal you kept as you had conversations with individuals.

- If you were to meet with some of these people together, what would the settings or arenas look like?

- How would you invite them? What would you actually say?

- Determine how you would open such a gathering, and three questions you would most like to ask such a group.

- During the next six weeks, host a gathering of three to five people. Move through the preparations you have made for that gathering.

- Following the gathering, make notes on your experience of it. Also, evaluate and make revisions as needed with the questions you asked and the process you followed.

- Repeat this process every six weeks with three to five other people.

- After 12 to 18 months, note who is beginning to emerge as people to be invited to a core team gathering.

- Plan for this initial core team gathering, set a date, and extend invitations. State the purpose of the first meeting and the long-term goal.

As your core team forms, consider how the group will bond, establish trust, and create a sense of teamwork. Explain that the purpose of the core team is to guide the church in the process of redevelopment. Involve the group in determining what they need as they prepare to do this work. Some suggestions might include:

- creating a description of how they want to function together as a group
- engaging in a Bible study together
- engaging in a study about redevelopment and change
- sharing their faith stories
- exploring the spiritual disciplines together, such as trying different prayer forms or fasting together
- list other ways to become acquainted and build trust

Chart a Course

Are you ready now to move forward in forming a core team? Is God calling you to this next step? If so, review the suggested process above and then determine what you will do to move forward. Write down your plan as clearly as possible, include a tentative time frame, and begin!

As you move through a year or more of forming a core team, you will draw together a community of people who are becoming more and more anxious to look at God's vision for the church. But during that time, keep the group focused on nurturing the sense of holy urgency, and the ongoing personal transformation in each person. Another temptation will be to engage in planning programs or activities that someone is excited about. The challenge will be to continue to form and shape the group by listening to the inner transformation taking place in each person and trusting that this will guide the group.

Looking Ahead

You are now experiencing what you envisioned in your guided meditation—a place where God's vision is fulfilled for a group that relates with and that nurtures one another. As a group, you are laying the foundation for welcoming an emerging vision for your church.

NOTES

1.   Marcus Buckingham and Donald O. Clifton, *Now Discover Your Strengths* (New York: The Free Press, 2001), is one resource to help individuals identify their personal strengths. An alpha-numeric code good for a one-time administration of an online survey accompanies the book. The survey identifies the individual's top five strengths from among 34. Another option is, Christian A Schwartz, *The Three Colors of Ministry: A Trinitarian Approach to Identifying and Developing Your Spiritual Gifts* (St. Charles, Ill.: Church Smart Resources, 2001).

2.   Only individuals who give themselves to deep change in their own lives are able to lead organizations through deep change. That is the central theme of Robert E. Quinn, *Deep Change* (San Francisco: Jossey-Bass Publishers, 1996).

3

Welcoming an Emerging Vision

Observations from a Mentor

With a group of committed companions who share a sense of holy urgency, the next step is to welcome an emerging vision. A vision in an embryonic stage drew you forward from the first day you began this journey. God was calling you to a new future and you indeed had some sense of that call. You knew deep within that God had something in mind both for you and for your church. You felt a sense of urgency flowing out of your concern for the lives and souls of people. Nudged by their own sense of urgency, others said yes to being your companions on this journey.

Vision Given by God

The holy longings in the hearts and minds of the core team are beginning to form clearer pictures. Some teams may find a specific visioning process useful; others simply allow time for common themes to emerge. The pace and timing of the process cannot be controlled; it differs from what most are used to. The timing for the vision to gain clarity is God's timing.

Crucial in the process is the recognition that the vision for a church comes from God. God works through individuals but it is ultimately God's vision that you are seeking. It is a vision that is given to you and that you welcome, rather than one you create. The major task of the core team at this point is to be open to what God is giving.

The process takes time. It takes time to listen to and to honor everyone. On the core team both long-time members and people new to the church have a voice. It takes time to listen to those voices and explore what is deep within people. It takes time to listen to God, to discern how God is leading. It is hard work for some—hard to resist the temptation to rush ahead and get on with the "real" work of redevelopment. But no work lasts for long unless the work flows out of a commonly owned, clear vision.

The temptation for some will be to pull out a vision developed some years ago. Why not? Dust off that work; change a few words to make it sound more up to date. Or another temptation: simply affirm the catchy words and phrases of articulate persons, persons for whom appropriate words just roll off their tongues. Or the team might want to honor and adopt the thoughts and words of the pastor. Resist all those temptations to make this part of the process move along more quickly and more easily. For a vision to have power it must come from the deep places within the lives and longings of people. Birthed by God, the vision comes through the hearts and souls of people. It is a product of feelings and passions as well as thinking.

Function of a Vision

The pictures, the dreams, the images we carry in our heads function as a magnet, pulling us into their fulfillment. A vision becomes a self-fulfilling prophecy. A clear, compelling vision has the power to draw us into a new reality. Vision sustains us in hard and troubled times, reminding us of the purpose behind our work. And the vision has even more sustaining power as we remember that the vision is God's desire and plan for us, not merely our own desires. The vision is no more than powerless window dressing unless it has emerged from deep and strong God-given passions.

During redevelopment, life in the congregation can become chaotic. Change calls for new responses and new directions. Old patterns and norms are changing. New paths are developed to take you to new places. Worship styles frequently shift. Staff may increasingly focus on equipping persons new in the faith. Established members may depend more on each other for nurture and support rather than staff. Expectations about appropriate dress change. The familiar disappears.

Vision serves as a compass, giving a sense of direction when people feel lost. It serves as a gyroscope keeping the church steady in the midst of turbulence. Without a clear, powerful vision, people become disoriented with no sense of how to move forward.

Focusing on the future God has in mind holds the church steady and provides guidance as decisions are made. The atmosphere of a committee or board meeting changes dramatically when the group focuses on the purpose for change. Attention shifts from the desires of individuals to what serves the vision.

Three Central Questions

Let's get down to some practical processes, some of the actual ways the core team becomes aware of the vision God has for the church. God's vision does finally find the people rather than the people finding a vision; however, there are important, practical things that can open a church to God's vision for them. Three questions are central: Who are we? Who is our neighbor? Why are we here? These three questions provide a practical framework. Each question plays a critical role.

Who are we? Who are we historically as a church in this place? Later, the core team will have these conversations with the entire congregation. But for now, explore with the core team what your best days were like? When were they? What years? What was going on in the church? What were your values? What was your relationship with the broader community? What was happening in peoples' lives?[1]

Different memories emerge. Some remember a time when statistically the church flourished. Others remember a difficult time when people faithfully faced adversity. Others focus on a prophetic role the church took. In the diversity of memories, look beyond the statistics and activities. Search for the common elements, the values and commitments that were being lived out.

Outward versus Inward Focus

Just as individuals are created in the image of God, churches are created and planted by God with an essence that is healthy and whole. That essence is outward focused. As it develops, the outward-focused church lives out its mission of offering the life-giving gospel to people. Interaction with the community molds ministries. An inner passion for the well being of others guides the development of the church.

Over the years the church's focus frequently turns inward. Concern for its own well being replaces concern for people beyond the church.

Survival replaces mission. The goal in redevelopment is exactly that, re-development, a return to the work of that initial development stage. Redevelopment does not ask a church to be different from its essential identity. Redevelopment is reconnecting with who you are at your core. The goal is to allow that healthy and whole essence to mold life as people discern how to fulfill God's purpose for their church. Basic to seeing what God has in mind today is recalling what God had in mind when the church was first planted.

Begin to reflect on what would be going on in the church if the values affirmed in the best days were still central to all decision making. Recall the relationship of the church with the community then and imagine today's version of that relationship. Living in ways that affirm those values and developing relationships grounded in those values will take the church well into redevelopment. Redevelopment, the change called for, takes the church to a different place from where it is today. But it reconnects the church with its historical essence.

Exceptions do exist. A church planted some years ago may never have flourished statistically or missionally. Churches are planted that never live out of God's purpose for them. An inward focus rather than an outward focus shapes the core. That church may need to give itself to a new church start process. Redevelopment may not be the right journey. The denominational support person can help in this decision.

Getting to Know the Neighborhood

The second question: Who is our neighbor? Vital ministry connects who the church is and what it has to offer, with the needs and opportunities beyond it. Churches often assume they know who is out there in the broader community, what their needs are, and the opportunities for connecting with them. Assumptions form without research. But a commitment to live in an outward-focused way, giving priority to persons beyond the walls of the church, makes it imperative to abandon the assumptions and actually get to know them.

How do you learn who your neighbor is? How do you learn about their needs, their hurts, their longings? No one way suffices. A core team creatively uses its imagination. Acquire and look at formal demographic information as a first step after you define your primary parish boundaries. The team can then build on that basic demographic information through direct, personal approaches to people in the neighborhood.

One church organized Saturday block walks. With the primary objective of getting to know the neighborhood, they knocked on doors and asked a few simple questions. The church began to know the neighborhood and the neighborhood began to know the church. Over the span of a couple of years, the geographical parish was covered.

Members of another church spent time in their neighborhood coffeehouse being open to conversations that emerged. Other churches assigned blocks to individuals to watch for persons moving in and out. Contacts were made quickly with new people.

Nothing substitutes for firsthand, face-to-face information gathering. In face-to-face encounters, relationships are developed that influence both the church members and the neighbors. Individuals begin to be known rather than labeled or categorized according to appearances. Amazing things begin to happen as people connect with people. God begins to use these connections to plant new visions and dreams.

The importance of the diversity of strengths among core team members becomes clearer. Some have strengths equipping them for face-to-face contacts. Others have strengths for other areas of research or for preparation of resources. Honor each person and use their strengths in ways that are fulfilling for the individual and useful for the mission of the church.

Why Are We Here?

With some understanding of who you are and who your neighbor is, you are ready for that third question: Why are we here? And at this point, resist the strong temptation to immediately engage in action. Some will want to jump to asking: "How can who we are be used to meet the needs of people? What are the activities and programs we can create?" During the process of redevelopment, slow down the persons who want to rush ahead into activities they feel implement the emerging vision. What is needed first is time simply to listen to God.

And how do you listen to God—how do you discern God's will? Biblical material and theological reflections on the church's mission are important. These resources prepare people to open themselves up to listen, and discernment listening is hard for some. It takes time. But take the time. Take time individually and in groups. Take time and talk with each other about what you are hearing. Take time to hear each other. Take time now or it will take forever.

As you are opening up to discern God's vision for your church, remember the urgency felt for people and their lives. Remember the whole person and not only the physical or only the spiritual needs. The vision God has for your church is different from the vision God has for a social service agency or for a pastoral counseling service. The vision may include some of what you find in other places. But God has a vision of whole people, fully living as sons and daughters of God.

Describing the Future with Longing and Passion

How do you know when you have finally found a compelling vision, or more accurately, when a compelling vision has found you? The test is not whether something can be chiseled in stone in 25 words or less. The test is whether people are able to talk with each other about what their church will look like several years from now. Can they describe the feel, the taste, who is there, and what is happening in their lives?

People claimed by a compelling vision describe the future with a longing and passion in their voices. Energy rises in them as they talk. They are clearly people on a mission that is given to them from beyond. They are hopeful people compelled into action.

You will reach the point where a compelling vision has been found and a compelling vision has found you. You may be saying, "How long does this visioning process take? We don't have forever to get through this." The reality is that it does take a long time. It takes many structured and unstructured conversations. The core team first has the conversations. In the next chapter, the journey moves on to include a widening circle of participates. Out of those conversations something emerges that has form— something that begins to be experienced as God given.

Reflections of a Companion

Who are we? Who is our neighbor? Why are we here? These simple questions surfaced again and again in the core team. The questions focused us. Their answers guided us. They were more effective in helping us discern God's vision for our church than any book we read or training we attended.

Initially, I thought that I would arrive at Valley View Church and spend a year listening to the people and getting to know the neighborhood and the community. Then, having gleaned all that wisdom, I would utter a sentence that clearly and exactly captured the vision to which God was calling us. The people would hear it and instantly rise to their feet with a fervent, "Yes!" and off we would go. We would see it in one moment and become it in the next.

It was a nice fantasy. Maybe it has happened that way for some folks; it just did not happen that way for us. Our experience felt more like a birthing. Our vision arrived like an infant. All the pieces and parts were there, but it took time and tending for it to grow into maturity.

An Ongoing Task

Like nurturing a sense of holy urgency and developing a core team, once we began trying to discern a vision, discernment became part of our ongoing work. We did not "do" vision and then move on to something else. Discerning God's vision for us became a normal and regular part of our life together. Who are we? Who is our neighbor? Why are we here? Even after the redevelopment was anchored, we were still asking those questions and refining the vision. The general direction of it did not change, but with each year the picture of where we were heading got clearer and more focused. Later, those questions ensured we stay adaptive to shifts in our congregation and our environment.

One of our visions was an active ministry to and with the many youth in our neighborhood. In the beginning, it existed only in our imaginations. As the years went by, however, that vision moved from being something that we dreamed in our heads and wrote about on paper to something that we lived. We progressed from talking about what it would be like to impact the lives of youth, to four years later knowing youth whose lives had been changed because of the church. The more we saw and experienced concrete manifestations of the vision, the fuller and more compelling it became.

The Vision Is God's

In the discernment process, the deepest shift came in our understanding of whose vision it was. We started the journey thinking that we were looking for our vision. Midway through the process we realized that the vision we longed for was God's. God's vision entailed connecting our passions with the world's needs.

For us, it happened like this.

Listening

The first question that needed to be addressed was "Who are we?" As I had originally planned, listening was my focus that first year and I listened every way I could think of. My goal was to hear people's hopes and dreams and understand their passions. I visited individuals in their homes, met with people in small groups, and posed questions and invited response through e-mail and letters. And so did members of the core team.

Listening was no longer just the pastor's job. While I pursued it officially, core team members went about it more informally, chatting with friends over coffee and asking questions on the golf course. We had talked with each other about what mattered most to us. Now we were curious about what other people in the church valued.

Unearthing Buried Passions

For me, mining for passions and values looked like this. When I heard a value expressed or a dream lifted up, I would affirm it, "Boy, Avery, it sounds like you care about people becoming involved with mission in hands-on ways." People let me know when I heard them correctly and when I did not. My goal was to listen and hear the depth of what they were trying to convey, so my job was to get curious.

Sometimes what I heard sounded on the surface like a longing to preserve the status quo. In those instances particularly, I had put myself in my "curious place" and dug around to see if there was something deeper driving it.

Elena from the core team and I were driving to a meeting with Ada one spring Saturday. For 22 minutes we listened to Ada lambaste the 10-year-old "new" hymnal and bemoan the loss of the old hymns in worship. She went on and on.

Initially, we both wanted to move her off the topic. But if we had, we never would have heard her real concern. Fortunately, we resisted our initial impulse and gently questioned her as to why the old hymns meant so much to her. We learned that they were the songs sung when she experienced conversion as a teenager. She had sung them at various key points in her life, and that music reminded her of the realness of God in a way that nothing else did. She wanted to maintain that kind of close-to-God experience for herself and she wanted it for others too. Underneath it all, she valued music as a way of experiencing God. The task was to help Ada extend that deep value into a future vision, a vision consistent with who we were as a church.

Elena shared about her granddaughter's experience at church camp. She had come home somehow different and with a CD that she played over and over again. Elena wondered if her granddaughter's experience was somehow like Ada's. As we talked, Ada's vision expanded from a worship service where people all sang the same hymns, to a worship service where music helped all people experience the holy presence of God. She ultimately became a supporter of the contemporary worship service we were thinking of adding. And later, when a new hymnal supplement came out, her comments helped others understand the need for a new generation to have music that has meaning for them.

Surfacing deeply held values was the key to unlocking this first step towards a vision. Individuals in the church had values that shaped their attitudes and behaviors, but what about the church itself? Did it as an organization hold particular values that could be seen from generation to generation?

Sharing the Fun

The core team decided early on that it did not want to do this vision work in isolation. They found creative ways that the entire church could take part. As a way of listening for the values of our church as an entity, the core team members and I hosted a "wall of history" event one Saturday.[2] We invited everyone from the church to come and share his or her part of Valley View's history. Forty-three people came. They sat at tables, grouped by the decade they had arrived at the church. On newsprint, each group brainstormed and listed pertinent memories from that time. Who were the pastors and the lay leaders? What was going on in the city, nation, and world at that time? What were the main ministries of the church? For what was the church known in the community? What were the primary challenges the church faced in that decade? "Do not worry if you are not exactly sure about the exact details," we encouraged. "Put down what you remember."

We had seven tables spanning seven decades. It was fascinating to watch. Some tables worked quietly, others were raucous. When all were done the tables took turns relating their part of the church's history. The oldest group, who had been part of Valley View since the 1930s, went first. They taped their newsprint on the wall and talked about what the church was like in that era. Decade by decade we spread our history in front of us. By the end, the history of Valley View belonged to us all.

With it spread before us on the wall, we sat back and looked at the sweep of our history. We searched for values and themes that were common across the entire history of the church. Every decade had shared something about ministry with children and youth. In the 1940s, the church had turned the basement into a roller skating rink. A preschool had been started in the '60s. The early '80s were remembered for the adopt-a-grandchild program. Having the story on the wall helped us step back and see it from a new and more objective perspective. The church itself had values, and we discovered that children and youth were among its values. People noticed too that warmly welcoming newcomers to the community had been a hallmark of every generation, and so had social activism. What did that mean for us in this decade?

Together we reached the conclusion that the future into which we seemed to be heading was fully consistent with our past. The deeply rooted values and inherent strengths simply needed a new form appropriate for this new era. From that perspective, turning the fellowship hall into a coffeehouse for youth was not much different than putting a roller skating rink in the basement. That was an important "aha" for both the older members of our church who had begun to feel a bit marginalized, and the newer members of the church who were beginning to feel a bit stifled. Our future and our past were not in competition, but inextricably linked.

The deepest insights that day did not come out of my mouth or the mouths of the core team members, but out of the others who had come. Our think tank grew sevenfold that day. Now more people were pondering the basic questions. Large group gatherings like that provided venues for a common vision to emerge and be owned.

Discovering our Neighborhood

After we had a pretty good sense of who we were, we began to address the question "Who is our neighbor?" I chatted with people in the community to find out about the city and its needs. The principal of the high school, small business owners, a popular beautician, a bus driver, coordinators of the community social service agencies—each saw a different slice of the community. Each was an invaluable source of information. The core team was a great place to share my learnings and hear their responses. Disagreement with what a principal had told me about the ethnic makeup of our surrounding neighborhood prompted them to start investigating things too. The core team and I gathered and reviewed demographic information about the area surrounding the church. Some of the information it contained did not seem to jive with our experience, so we followed it up by looking for ourselves to see if it was accurate.

What we found excited us. We invited speakers involved with various aspects of the community to bring us a "mission moment" during worship. During those brief moments, the entire congregation heard about our community's struggle with poverty, hunger, literacy, and prejudice. And while that was not news to anyone in the sanctuary, placing it in the context of worship and introducing the topic with appropriate scripture proclaimed that it was not just something that concerned us, it was something that concerned God.

One way in which Valley View helped both youth and adults step beyond the doors of the church and learn about their community was through a scavenger hunt created by our youth director. Church members spent an afternoon in the central business district locating parks and low-income apartment buildings. They counted restaurants and benches and services provided at the neighborhood health clinic. They found out how much it cost to rent a room and were surprised to discover that there is no bus service in our city on Sundays. "I've lived here almost all my life," mused one woman. "Why didn't I know those things?"

Discovering Our Purpose

Only after learning something about ourselves and our neighborhood did we begin addressing the "Why are we here?" question. We utilized different visioning tools and techniques, and found that one of the most helpful exercises was simply imagining the future church. This was done first with the core team and then later with the congregation during a worship service. We imagined walking back into the building 10 years in the future. "Imagine that Valley View is everything you ever dreamed of. . . . What do you see? What do you hear?" People were very concrete about naming what was going on in that longed-for church—the sounds of children; variety in skin color and language; people laughing, studying, praying; links to community services. It was a place of spiritual formation and of service that empowered both the one serving and the one served.

A compelling vision of our future self energized us as the initial urgency created by crisis dwindled away. By this point into the effort, the roof was sound, the finances were close to being under control, and there was a slowly growing segment of children and young adults. In many respects, things were fixed. It would have been easy at that point for people to settle back and say we had arrived. The will-our-church-live urgency that had pervaded the church when I first arrived had been replaced by a general sense of satisfaction among the people. A compelling vision of what could be was the only thing that continued to keep us moving.

Which Way Is the Energy Flowing?

Yet even into the fourth year the church seemed most motivated by the aspect of the vision that said, "What's in it for us?" Though the vision certainly lifted up the needs resident in the community, what still resonated most strongly for people was the end result of strengthening the church and improving their own experience. Members would comment during coffee hour, "I see the children and I know that our church is going to be OK." "It's so nice to once again come away from church feeling good."

I appreciated the positive comments, but they signaled something about our spiritual health. Our energy was still focused primarily on improving things for ourselves. Our vision would not be mature, or more truly, we would not be mature in it, until the focus of our energy was turned outward.

We needed our very hearts to be redeveloped. We had started with a life-and-death concern about the church. Our goal was achieving a life-and-death concern for those that the church was called to serve.

That shift began with a churchwide series of home gatherings based on the book of Revelation and the seven letters God wrote to the seven churches.[3] We began the time by inviting people to share their own personal visions for the church. Then we read the seven letters written to the seven churches, discussed the passages, and pondered the questions, "What would God write to us?" "For what would we be commended?" "How would we be challenged?" "What was God's vision for our church?" There was no hesitation in their voices. God did have an opinion about our church and a vision for it and from that time, our vision moved from something that was about us, to something about what God was doing in the world through us. That was a radical shift for us.

What strengths has your congregation been gifted with? What are the pressing needs of your community? How would God love to use you? God has a plan for your church. Blessings as you and your church begin to discover that plan.

Guidance from a Coach

What is a vision for a church? A vision is a description of a common picture that people have for their future together. It describes in general terms the way they understand that God wants them to be and live. A vision helps a group to move in a common direction, therefore having an important aligning function. And perhaps most important, a vision connects all the pieces of the sense of holy urgency that have emerged from within individuals, and gives them a unified sense of meaning and purpose. The pieces come together. There is a meshing—a rhythm to what is emerging from God. A well-grounded vision, clearly stated, is so compelling that people are motivated to move toward that picture of God's desired future for them.

As you have spent time with the core team, you may have caught glimpses of the emerging vision that God is calling your church to. In this coaching section we will focus on this vision and begin designing the ways in which the core team will welcome and support its emergence. This is a gradual and intentional process. You will discover what God has in mind for the church as a whole by learning about what God is stirring up in individuals.

Reflect and Journal

The goal for this coaching session is for the core team to develop a plan for discerning and welcoming the emerging vision God has for your church. As you prepare to begin work on this goal, take some time to reflect on the following questions and record your responses in your journal.

- What are your initial thoughts and feelings about engaging in this discernment process?

- What excites you about the discernment process?

- What frightens you about the discernment process?

- What glimpses of a vision are you starting to see?

- What are the sources and groundings for these glimpses? From whom are they coming? How frequently are they being expressed?

Develop a Plan

As the core team develops a plan, there are three basic questions that need to be addressed to create the framework in which to sense God's vision: Who are we? Who is our neighbor? Why are we here? The previous mentor and companion sections provide insight and practical suggestions for ways to proceed. This section builds on those ideas.

1. First, determine how the core team will listen to what people might share in response to the question, "Who are we?" What existing settings might be used? (Examples: study classes, committee meetings, small groups, etc.) What settings need to be created? Who will be present? How will people be invited? What specific questions will you ask? (See mentor and companion sections for examples of questions to ask.)

2. Next, determine how the core team will listen for what people might share in response to the question, "Who is my neighbor?" Additionally, what other practical research steps may need to be taken to fully answer this question? (Examples: demographic and census information—usually available from your local chamber of commerce, direct conversations in the neighborhood, discussions at the local coffeehouse, etc.)

3.   Finally, determine how the core team will listen for what people might
      share in response to the question, "Why are we here?" Listen for
      ways in which the senses of holy urgency begin to connect in their
      reflections on this question.

As you focus on these three questions, remember that this process
takes time. In the initial phase of this process, a sense of the vision may
start to emerge in a few months, but the clarifying process will take years,
and actually continues forever as God continues to reveal additional aspects
of a vision to the people.

Chart a Course

Now it is time for the core team to design a plan for listening for the vision
God has given to your people. Determine the process you will follow and
the details of that process to address questions 1–3 above. Be as specific
as possible, and include a time frame whenever possible—and delight in
the journey of discovery you are about to engage in.

After you have been engaged in this process for approximately three
months, reflect with the core team about:

•   What is this experience like for us?

•   What are our learnings?

- Where do we need to make shifts in our process?

How will you know when you have actually surfaced the vision God has in mind for your church? Again, by listening and observing. People will begin to talk with greater passion about the future they want to be a part of. People will begin to behave in ways that are increasingly consistent with the vision. People will be expressing a longing to be part of that vision. Some people, primarily the core team, will seem to own and be owned by the vision.

Looking Ahead

When God's vision for your church has been identified, how do you assist an ever-increasing number of people to own and be owned by the vision? Chapter 4 addresses this question.

NOTES

1. Roy M. Oswald and Robert E. Friedrich, Jr., *Discerning Your Congregation's Future: A Strategic and Spiritual Approach* (Bethesda, Md.: The Alban Institute, 1996), 64–75, presents a design for "An Evening of Historical Reflection." The process would be especially useful as the core team engages the broader congregation in remembering their historical roots.
2. Ibid.
3. See pages 51–54 in *Discerning Your Congregation's Future* for instructions on running this type of home meeting.

4

Owning and Being Owned by the Vision

Observations from a Mentor

Many people find themselves entering this fourth stage of the process sometime between the 36- to 42-month mark. Across time, the vision increasingly becomes clear for the core team: they begin to own the vision and also begin to feel owned by it. A force beyond themselves draws them forward into something new and compelling. They are ready to move into action, but an essential task challenges them before the entire congregation can begin to act with passion and energy.

At this point, the core team is alone. They have little chance of succeeding if they jump into the ministry activities of redevelopment by themselves. The vision, even though clear to the core team, is not clear to the rest of the church. They have not experienced what the core team has. The people in the congregation do not yet own nor are they owned by the vision.

Challenge Greater than Communicating Words and Information

The challenge is greater than simply communicating the vision or educating people about the vision. Reaching the point where everyone has something memorized is not enough; rather, the goal is to reach the point where nothing can prevent people from moving into that future which God has in mind for them. The vision burns within them—a desire that will not allow them to sit still. It is connected with their deepest values and desires. But to reach that point requires planning and openness by the core team.

A compelling sense of holy urgency provided the foundation early in the journey. That urgency keeps the process moving. A core team gathered and gave themselves to the careful, soul-searching, and discerning work of visioning. They modeled and embodied the future, providing a foretaste for themselves and others. Now the core team, claimed by the vision, must bring the entire congregation into the process; however, inviting others to participate challenges the core team because it means welcoming the insights of others. The team extends the opportunity to influence future directions to everyone.

Although they are sometimes useful, visioning retreats alone do not accomplish the results. One church attempted several retreats during a two-year period. The energizing process left people on a high, but nothing changed in the church. No actions resulted. The plans from the retreats reflected the best thinking of the people but were not rooted in the passions of the hearts.

People needed time to personally reflect on the questions: Who are we? Who is our neighbor? Why are we here? They needed an extended period of time for reflection rather than a few hours at a retreat. Without that opportunity, the best that could be expected was simply for others to know someone else's vision in their heads. To provide the time needed, 12 months were then set aside for conversations in small groups. No notes were taken or compiled. First, the questions "Who are we?" and "Who is our neighbor?" were asked. Then, people were asked to respond to the question "What do you sense God is calling us to be as a church and how does your personal call fit into that?"

A compelling vision began to take shape. The vision had many similarities with the vision that had emerged for the core team. It also had shifted, reflecting now the passions and longings of other participants in the process. How it happened is not clear; but in time, people were clear that five years from then they would see their church as a church that people in the neighborhood talked about, and a church known for caring about the people in the community. Eventually, these pieces of the vision were stated more specifically: "We are a people who weave together this neighborhood into a place of justice, compassion, and wholeness by living out God's command to love God and neighbor."

A Permeating Vision

With the vision permeating the whole church organization, energy and focus is present. An increasing number of people embody the vision and values affirmed in their lives. The vision guides their thinking and actions as they interact with others. The church begins moving on a missional rather than a maintenance path, attracting more people. Proposals for change are received as life-giving opportunities. The strong sense of the call of God to the whole church claims the loyalty of all the groups. People experience being energized by a sense of purpose, mission, and movement. The goal is nothing less than the vision permeating all parts of the church.

How long does it take for the vision to permeate the whole system? Some churches reach that point more quickly than others. After the core team has allowed itself to be owned by a vision, it takes at least another 18 to 24 months for a major portion of the congregation to claim a vision and for the vision to claim all parts of the church. Not everyone will understand and embrace the vision. But with the vision effectively embodied by people, new participants in the church quickly understand the values and direction of the church.

Embodying the Vision

As the core team talks about the vision, they also live in ways consistent with the vision. Their actions, as well as their words, express and demonstrate the future reality to which God is leading. Words are important, but a life that reflects and demonstrates that new reality speaks powerfully. And life that passionately embodies a new reality serves as an invitation and a magnet. Through their example, the core team invites others to live into being an embodiment of the vision. By watching and interacting with the team, people begin to want for themselves the energy and joy they sense in the team. They reach that point where nothing can prevent them from moving into God's vision for them.

For example, if part of the vision is to be an inclusive community that reflects the demographics of the parish, the core team embodies that inclusivity. If part of the vision is a community where people are grounded in spirituality, core team members worship, pray, and develop relationships of accountability. Valuing individuals as beloved sons and daughters of God, they recognize the goodness in others. Each person is honored. With a vision of a community that invites persons into a life of discipleship, the core team models the inviting.

Opening Up the Process: Continual Formation of the Vision

Embodying the vision, in addition to talking about it, is important. But people have to be brought into a process very similar to the process that the core team itself went through. Opportunities for conversations, for sharing passions and personal dreams, are crucial. People need time to talk about what they sense is the future which God desires for the church.

I can hear your response now. But are we not the leadership team? We went through all of that. We carefully discerned God's will for this church, so why not simply bring others into a deep knowledge of that vision through words and demonstrations?

The process used by the core team allows individuals to open themselves to discover the vision God wants to give to them, rather than the vision coming from the pastor or another individual. It is important to continue the same principle for an ever-widening group of people, engaging them in the vision discernment process. Now you can begin to get a sense of why this part of redevelopment will take many months.

How is visioning done? It is done in as many ways as there are core teams and churches; however, some basic principles exist. Engage people in dialogue about the directions in which God seems to be calling the church. Use scripture passages to ground the discussions. Central to all gatherings is honoring all the people present—everyone's input is valued and respected. Team members open themselves to hearing God speak in new ways through the people present. God spoke through the individuals in the core team as an initial vision was emerging. God will continue to speak through individuals in the ongoing exploration and discussion.

The core team will be challenged to stay open and will be curious to see how God is expanding and enriching the vision as others are brought into the discussion. Core team members talk about how they have been claimed by the vision. They talk about and demonstrate the importance of the vision in their own lives. But they also carefully listen to people throughout the church to hear the passions that others have and what is deep within them. These two-way conversations contribute to what continues to emerge more fully as God's will for the church.

Public Articulation

Provide a few minutes in a variety of settings for people to share their dreams for the future of the church. Worship services, committee meetings, and study groups all offer opportunities. Those dreams begin to paint the picture of what the people sense to be that new and emerging reality for their church. The pictures depict what is happening as the church lives out its reason for being in the place where God has planted it. The values affirmed are evident as the church interacts with its broader community. In the pictures, people see who we are, who our neighbors are, and why we are here.

The more specific the picture, the better. What are the sounds, the smells, the feelings, and the images that will be present when the future has become the now? Those images stimulate the imaginations of others and stir desires within them. An emerging picture invites people to add their own contributions to the richness of the images.

The challenge to the core team is always to allow for participation by others. Not only do core team members want to influence others, but they are open to being influenced themselves. A core team member tells about her understanding of the vision and then invites another to add his understanding. And together they are always moving into a fuller understanding of the vision that God is communicating.

An Ongoing Process: Art not Science

Healthy churches engage in visioning on a regular basis, not once every four or five years. New realities continue to emerge, and they offer new opportunities and challenges. Visioning is an ongoing process that requires openness to embrace the always-emerging ways in which God calls. The church remains vital only as it continues to interact with God's emerging reality.

How does the core team know when the people own and are owned by the vision? How does the team know when it is time to start moving in specific, concrete ways toward the vision? When can you dare to make dramatic and visible changes? Listen carefully for members' answers to these questions during informal discussions. Do you hear people in ordinary conversation talk about hopes and dreams that are consistent with the vision? Listen carefully in meetings. Are issues and decisions approached in light of moving toward what is valued in the vision? Look at how you see people act. Are their actions increasingly congruent with the shifts the church is reaching for? Do you sense there are a sufficient number of people for whom nothing can hold them back from moving into the future for which God has in mind for the church?

Redevelopment in a congregation is always an art and not a science. No blueprint can be provided. No time line that is right in one setting is necessarily right in another. The next step, empowering people and removing barriers, allows the vision to move people forward into ministries. Avoid rushing through this step. It takes time for a large group of people to discern a commonly affirmed path. And do not be surprised if the broader vision differs somewhat from what you and the core team discussed. During this time, listen to how well people can talk about and interpret changes in light of the vision. How well do they understand new initiatives as part of a larger purpose rather than interesting novelty? You will know when it is time to move forward with new and specific strategies.

Reflections of a Companion

We were two-and-a-half years into the redevelopment process. The sense of holy urgency was growing, and an increasing percentage of the membership believed that God really was doing something in our midst. The congregation had a basic grasp of the church's strengths and values as well as a sense of the needs resident in the community. Our understanding of our purpose, though, our vision, was as hazy as a new Polaroid picture. The major elements were emerging, but details were still coming into focus.

As things began to move from the abstract towards the concrete, the core team and I felt we needed to expand the leadership base of the redevelopment effort. Much to our delight, the church council, the major decision and policy-making group in the church, eagerly joined us. Several of the core team members served on the church council. Their reports in those meetings had generated enthusiasm and support.

Listening for Common Themes

Together as a joint leadership team, we all listened carefully to the congregation. In large groups and small, in formal and informal gatherings, we continued to ask people to dream. People described their future church with great specificity: "I heard children laughing before I even walked in the door." "The signs for an upcoming dinner were written in three languages." "We commissioned a mission team in worship." Four themes or phrases surfaced again and again:

- ministering to and with children and youth
- welcoming diversity
- making a difference
- every member a minister

We heard these phrases over and over and when people spoke, there was an unmistakable energy in their voices. That is how the church council, core team, and I settled on those four themes as being the four key components of our vision. We believed the energy that accompanied them was a spiritual energy that signaled they were a critical part of our essential purpose. We quickly learned though that each person had his or her own idea about what those things meant. Stan's picture of making a difference was building a Habitat for Humanity house. Anna's picture was working to eliminate land mines. Both envisioned the church making a difference, but each saw it happening in a very different way. The more specific the people's visions were, the more energy they seemed to release. The joint leadership team welcomed that energy. It felt good and signaled that people's deep passions were being engaged. We did not anticipate the ramifications though, and were shocked when the energy manifested itself as conflict.

Clarity through Conflict

Some of the visions people had were compatible with each other even though the specifics were different. Stan's and Anna's ideas of how the church should make a difference did not compete with each other, though they were very different. One did not necessarily preclude the other; room existed for both. But not all visions were compatible—some collided.

In our city, no church openly welcomed gays and lesbians. A sizable portion of the congregation believed God's vision for us was to see them as no different than anyone else and invite and welcome them as beloved brothers and sisters in Christ. A smaller but much-loved and well-respected group of people had a different vision for the church that was just as compelling to them. They too heard God calling us to welcome gays and lesbians, but for the purpose of helping them transform their sexual orientation. Both felt a holy urgency around their vision that was strong and deep, but there was no reconciling the specifics of these visions.

I absolutely believe that the conflict that surfaced around this issue was ultimately positive and productive. We would not be the church we are today if we had shied away from it. The vision had to have flesh-and-blood specifics if it was to live and breathe. No church can be all things to all people. Our work in this part of redevelopment was nailing down the specifics of our purpose. Though the church leaders and I knew from our studying that significant conflict would inevitably arise at some point during the redevelopment process, this blindsided us. When it came, it came fast and hard—and it hurt everybody.

One Saturday morning two weeks before Easter, I finished my morning jog, made coffee, and sat down to leisurely enjoy the newspaper. I read the news, perused the sports scores, and then turned to the religion section. The headline hit me like a punch in the stomach.

In response to events of that time, a minister friend and I had felt called to take a personal stance supporting the ordination of gays and lesbians into ministry. We invited other like-minded pastors to join us for a small prayer gathering, and then opened it up to others in the community who wanted to participate. We made it clear that the gathering was not sponsored by any group or church; rather, we were simply concerned individuals coming together for prayer and a symbolic gesture of support.

We had decided to hold the event in a park precisely to downplay any connection with a particular church. Earlier in the week, a reporter had called and asked me some questions. "Where does your church stand on this?" she asked. I replied that the people held very different opinions and varied widely in their stance. The congregation was not of one mind, I said. This was not a church action.

And yet, the headline that morning read, "Local Church to Lead Show of Support for Homosexuals." The article went on to say that Valley View Church under my leadership was planning the gathering. I was furious. For this misquote did not just affect me, it affected the entire church.

As I sat there at the table, my heart ached for the church. We had worked so hard to build a climate of trust where different voices and opinions were honored. It was common knowledge in the church that the membership did not hold a common stance in regard to this issue. But we had, up to this point, respected each other's opinions as we studied and discussed it. Our church would not take a stand, either way, until all were in agreement.

Now all I could imagine was people's sense of betrayal as they read the paper. All I could see was everything we had worked so hard for suddenly falling apart. We had come so far in this redevelopment journey. Would this kill it? I felt sick as I thought about facing the congregation in worship the next morning. It was one of the longest days of my life.

A Defining Moment

The next morning, the church was packed and the mood was tense. I was terrified. The worship service began with the call to worship and the opening hymn. Then I abandoned the planned order of worship. I spoke very briefly, less than five minutes, outlining the situation and sharing my feelings about it.

Then I asked what this was like for them. We followed the Quaker way—beginning in silence and then letting silence precede and follow each spoken thought. The following 50 minutes are among the most holy I have ever experienced. Frightening? Yes. Painful? Yes. But incredibly holy. Rising from the silence, people stood and spoke, trembling voices betraying deep emotion. A holy presence pervaded the room as each person's story and opinion was heard and honored.

It was a defining moment for us as a church. A critical piece of our vision came into focus. Though we gained no further clarity that day about the church's response to gays and lesbians, we knew now that we would be a church that agreed to disagree. Beyond what we believed about this issue, or any other, the church would welcome different voices and honor differing opinions. An important part of our vision was being a foretaste of the "kin-dom" of God. We would be a church of brothers and sisters who sought to live out a model of power "with" rather than power "over."

This level of specificity in the vision coupled with an experience of it, galvanized some and repelled others. Five families, now having a clearer understanding of the church's vision, determined it was incompatible with theirs. They made the difficult choice to leave the church and find another whose vision and values better matched theirs. It was the right decision and yet it was so painful. Some of them had been part of the church since childhood and were active in leadership. They had stayed faithful to the church in the difficult years when many others had left. They loved the church and the church loved them. But in the weeks that followed, the church leadership was clear; this is who they were and they could live no other way. They cried with those who were choosing to leave and blessed them as they left to find the church whose vision matched their own.

It ripped my heart out to know my actions had unwittingly triggered the conflict. It was so hard to watch these people I cared about leave. Yet, from that point on, the vision owned us much more deeply. I learned once again the gospel truth about the inextricable linkage between death and life. I died that day and again in the weeks following, and so did the joint leadership team. How appropriate for this to take place during Lent. Our love of control, security, and stability shattered into a thousand pieces. All we could do was turn to God. It was as transforming for us personally, as it was for the church corporately.

So I can talk about all the concrete ways that the leadership and I tried to listen for the vision that was emerging in our congregation and echo it back to the people, but for our church, nothing was as critical as the conflict. It forced us to address things we had managed to skirt around and ignore before. We could not claim who we were and who we were called to be until we were ready to be clear about who we were not. From that point on, the other aspects of the vision seemed to come into sharper focus.

The church council, core team, and I tried to share the emerging vision every way we could think of. It was not much different from my strategy for getting healthy food into my kids when they were young. Everything had to count. Even fun snacks had to have some nutritional element. We carried that same kind of obsessiveness into communicating the vision. Everything we did had to somehow communicate the vision of who we were called to become. The people themselves were naming it. Leadership's task was to notice when it was named or lived out and lift it up so that everybody could see it.

Sermons, newsletters, meetings—all were vehicles for telling the story. Our church newsletter came out weekly and after initially being horrified that I would have to come up with a weekly column, I realized that it was an incredible opportunity to lift up some aspect of our mission and vision

each week. Core team and church council members talked about the vision
in meetings they were a part of. A bulletin board encouraged people to
bring photographs that illustrated the different part of the vision.

Sharing the Vision through Word and Action

Perhaps even more important were the more subtle ways we communicated
the vision. My being and behavior, and that of the staff and the leadership,
had to embody the new way. We tried to live as though the vision of what
we were going to be someday was true right now, right here. The vision of
valuing children and youth led the core team to invite a high-school student
to join them. The vision of making a difference motivated the core team to
work together to clean up a nearby vacant lot that had become overrun
with weeds and trash. Our job was to be a concrete expression of the
vision. We wanted to be yeast, so that as people brushed up against us, they
too would catch the vision and become leaven for the people with whom
they came in contact. Our actions were as important as our words. How
we acted mattered; people watched.

Interestingly, and perhaps naturally, the ones who caught hold of the
vision the quickest were the newcomers. They chose the church partly
because of the vision that was being embodied by the core team and church
council. They did not know our history, and did not know that the vision was
a place we were heading towards rather than someplace we lived. Many
newcomers embodied the new culture. Their very presence helped support
the emerging vision and give flesh to it.

So that is what this part of the redevelopment process was like for me.
I learned that conflict was our friend, a difficult one perhaps, but a friend.
And I learned that when we let go of rigidity and control, when I let go, was
precisely the moment when God could work most powerfully.

God gifts each church with different strengths and thus with a different
purpose. A church that knows itself and knows its purpose is both powerful
and winsome. Blessings as you work with the coach to determine your
next steps in helping the vision permeate the system.

Guidance from a Coach

The core team guides the lengthy process of discovering the vision that has been planted deep within your church. You have the sacred privilege of listening to the sense of holy urgency that God speaks to each person. The core team hears people reflect on the three crucial questions of "Who are we?" "Who is our neighbor?" and "Why are we here?" With this feedback, you start to see the common threads of the vision that God desires for this faith community.

Once God's vision emerges, a core team needs to focus on how to help a broader base of people own and be owned by the vision. The process for listening to the inner leadings of additional people must be repeated constantly and consistently through many settings and methods. The leaders' actions need to be congruent with the vision. The vision needs to be simply stated and clear. Conflict, as was related in the companion section, needs to be anticipated. Whether it happens at this point in the process or a later one, it is inevitable.

Reflect and Journal

The goal for this coaching section is for the core team to develop a comprehensive plan for assisting people to own and be owned by the vision. As you read this goal, take a moment to reflect with the core team about your own sense of ownership of the vision. Then consider how much the vision owns you. How would you describe its claim on your life? Record your responses in your journal.

Develop a Plan

Review the suggested plan for achieving the goal above.

- Identify all of the planned, intentional opportunities and gatherings in which persons might be invited to describe their understanding of God's vision for the church—places where the core team can ask questions and listen. For example, schedule the first half hour of a church board meeting as a time for core team members to share their understanding of God's vision. Then invite others to offer their understandings. Encourage people to describe the vision in specific terms. Possible questions include:

1. If we were fully living into the vision God has for us, what would the atmosphere and mood be like here?

2. What attitudes would be prevalent?

3. How would people's lives be impacted?

4. What kind of energy would be generated?

5. What would the participants be telling their friends and neighbors?

6. What would be the sources of inspiration?

- Heighten the core team's ability to watch for spontaneous moments in which to invite input. For example, a core team member is part of a coffee-hour discussion, which includes comments about new worshipers who are in the process of learning English. The core team member could ask how the person making the observation sees this informing any of the three basic questions asked in the last chapter. Or, how might these new worshipers be part of God's vision for the church? It will be helpful for the core team to role-play possible spontaneous moments to invite input about the vision, such as coffee hour, committee meetings, church clean-up projects, and so forth.

- Record in your journal all occasions and occurrences of the two options above. Note where you might start to branch out in innovative ways from your most frequently used methods and mediums for inviting people into discovering and sharing their understanding of God's vision for the church. For example, if you note that existing small social groups within the church are not being used as places for gathering input about the vision, devise a plan for doing so.

- Compile a list of all communication avenues and resources in and around your church (examples: newsletter, e-mail, Web sites, signs, worship announcements, coffee-hour conversations, sermons, bulletin inserts, posters, etc.). Brainstorm ways that the core team can use these avenues to communicate their understandings of God's vision for the church, and invite others to respond with input about their understandings.

- Create frequent times of reflection for the core team members in which they can lift up what they are hearing, reflect on its meaning, and hear how God is calling them to recognize growth and shifts in the vision. For example, initially the vision may not have spoken about intentional ministry with singles, but changing trends on the surrounding neighborhood may now create that imperative.

- Help the core team to recognize that conflict will be an inevitable part of this process. Allow time to discuss how you intend to deal with conflict. Build your skills in that area. It will be helpful to have a skilled communications professional join some of your meetings. Ask this person to design some role-playing exercises to help the core team assist individuals when differences in understanding the vision occur. Work towards identifying the underlying values that people hold, which most likely are held in common but are being expressed in different ways.

- List other options for achieving this goal.

Chart a Course

Review the suggested plan above and decide on the steps you will take over time to help an increasing number of people to own and be owned by the vision God has for the church. Be specific in the plans you will commit to. As you begin to carry out that plan, listen for confirmation that others are owning and being owned by the vision God has planted in their hearts. Take time for the core team to recognize and celebrate that confirmation.

As you talk about the vision, note when you experience the most excitement and intensity. How is God speaking to you about the vision at these moments? Note when you experience the most complacency, fear, or disinterest in the vision. How is God speaking to you about the vision at these moments? Record these reflections in your journal.

Looking Ahead

A compelling vision will act as a magnet, drawing people to it. As people begin to own, and be owned by, the vision, they will be eager to live God's vision in concrete ways. Up to this point in the process, the work has focused on clarifying the vision. Now, as the vision continues to be refined, the core team begins empowering people to bring that vision to reality.

Empowering People and Removing Barriers

Observations from a Mentor

"The harvest is ready and the laborers are few." Those words of Jesus describe this stage of the redevelopment journey. Your work over the years has laid a good foundation and the harvest is ready. But to claim it, the line has to be crossed from wishful thinking into action. Crossing that line means empowering people and removing barriers so that they can get to work.

Trusting People

Empowering people requires three basic tasks from leadership: trusting people, connecting people, and equipping people.

If the core team had not trusted people, redevelopment would not have progressed this far. The resourcefulness, creativity, and wholeness of people were affirmed as they were brought into the vision process. God worked through the entire congregation in giving the vision for the future, and God continues to work through all the people, planting passions in their hearts. Those passions give energy for birthing new ministries.

Trusting people and freeing them to initiate ministries, however, can threaten committees used to exercising control. Encouraging words may well invite individual initiative. The actions of those committees, however, may convey something different when they require layers of bureaucratic review before granting approval for initiatives. Trusting people means stretching beyond mere words and opening the way for them to act. One woman, claimed by the vision of her church, discovered her passion to be responding to women diagnosed with breast cancer. She envisioned a new support group to help connect these women both with each other and with the assurance and hope found in the gospel message. Her church's policies, however, required her to get approval from the pastoral care committee, the women's ministry group, and the trustees before initiating her new ministry. Rather than allowing her passion to cool, she found a more welcoming setting for her ministry in another community organization.

Recognizing the need to streamline its process, another church adopted a policy that opened the way for new ministry initiatives. The policy authorized the pastor, in consultation with two of the key lay leaders, to approve any new ministry initiative brought by an individual. Limits were set. The openness did not give blanket approval for whatever a person might wish to pursue in the name of the church. The ministry had to be judged consistent with and supportive of the vision of the church. Simply to embrace whatever emerges from the passions of individuals is irresponsible if it jeopardizes the specific future to which God calls a church.

Connecting People

The second major part of empowering people involves connecting them with others who share a common passion for ministry. One church in the middle of a redevelopment journey experienced a pastoral change. Reflecting on what was needed from a new pastor, they identified the networking function. Their former pastor was excellent at helping people find the right ministry team in the church, the place where their strengths would be welcomed and utilized. They recognized the importance of connecting people with similar passions and interests and particularly did not want to lose that strength at this point in their redevelopment.

Another church regards every individual walking through their door as a gift from God. They see that discovering what the person brings to God's ministry is their responsibility. The new person is paired up with a member who serves as a companion for a year. One of the expectations in the relationship is discovering the gifts of the person and connecting the person with the right group where those gifts can be used in ministry.

Equipping People

Equipping people for ministry is a third major component of empowerment, and there are many aspects to this. One church believes that the best way it can equip people for ministry is through providing opportunities for continual spiritual formation. Their objective is to continually improve the opportunities for spiritual development.

The church annually monitors itself in three areas: passionate spirituality, inspiring worship, and holistic small groups. Do the people have a faith that leads to a strong conviction that God acts in powerful ways? Does the church offer worship where people experience the presence of God that leads to joyous exultation as well as quiet reverence? Do people participate in small groups that respond to their individual needs and help them develop their God-given gifts? Each year, a survey indicates the degree to which the church has moved forward in these areas. With the feedback from the annual survey, the church makes adjustments for improvements.[1]

Another area of focus for equipping is skill development. Some people have strong passion for a ministry area but have not yet developed the skills for the ministry. In one church, a person felt called to develop an after-school program for young children. She had strengths in engaging children in nurturing activities, but her skills in the area of organizing, recruiting, and motivating adults were weak. She was paired up with a mentor, someone who walked alongside her, helping her gain new skills in working effectively with adults.

Mentoring is a critical task for the redeveloping church. Persons new to the Christian faith may bring eagerness and enthusiasm. Developing their potential and equipping them with needed skills requires caring mentoring. As skills are developed, sometimes the tasks require more energy or commitment than anticipated. Equipping then takes the form of support and encouragement.

To move into their full potentials, individuals require different styles of mentoring. Some may need a lot of teaching and directing, where others may have the knowledge and skills but need support and encouragement. Still others may be both skilled and motivated and able to move into new ministry opportunities in fully competent ways. The core team is sensitive to what individuals need and responds appropriately in each situation.[2]

Organizational Barriers

To claim the harvest, barriers to empowerment must be removed. Two primary barriers are the way a church is organized and people who are resistant to change. Organizational barriers frequently receive the most attention. Often churches view their organizational structure as the main impediment to change. Reorganizing or restructuring is embraced as the answer to the problems they face. Churches invest great effort in changing the organizational structure. Sometimes that is helpful. Yet frequently churches experience no change except what can be seen on their organizational chart. They rearranged the structure, without changing how they behaved with each other. Reorganizing the structure can be an effective strategy to avoid the more difficult work of redevelopment.

Structure does need examining; however, no organizational structure is inherently good or bad. The important question is simply whether it works for you. Is it functional? Does it allow you to live into your vision? Does it encourage broad ownership while allowing timely decision making? Does it provide for openness to creativity? Make the changes you sense are needed. Be open to additional changes in the future as you continue to live into the vision. But, more important, be alert to other changes that may be needed in order for any church structures to be functional.

Human Barriers

Another barrier in the redevelopment journey is people who find change difficult. Sometimes these are people who early in the journey were enthusiastic. Sensing an urgency, they support what they see as hope for their church. But they remain focused on an urgency of crisis and fail to make the shift to a holy urgency. Remaining inward focused rather than becoming outward focused, their primary objective is to bring the church back to a place where survival is no longer threatened. Even as the rest of the congregation embraces the vision and the journey, they continue to value reestablishing and preserving the status quo.

Responding to the threat these individuals can present to the redevelopment journey is crucial. A person who is resistant to redevelopment often patiently waits, striking in a destructive way when the opportunity arises. A congregation may experience statistical growth for five or six years. Redevelopment may appear to be well along the journey and then, a small group within the church can bring the forward movement to a sudden stop.

One church with a 10-year pattern of gradual but steady growth experienced just such a reversal. The growth pattern in this small church had continued through two pastors, with worship attendance increasing steadily from 26 to 83. All the marks of redevelopment seemed present. New and younger families in the community had been welcomed into the church, and they had been brought into leadership. Lives were being changed through the outward focus of the church.

But a small group of long-time members and leaders experienced an increasing discomfort with the changes. They wanted back the church they had been previously comfortable with. And, with a change in pastors, they were able to recapture that church. In six months attendance dropped back to below 30. The appearances of redevelopment had been present but the barrier represented by people had not been adequately addressed.

Any element in the redevelopment journey not adequately addressed will eventually block the forward movement of the journey; for example, failure to develop an effective core team, a vision not truly owned broadly by the people in the church, or the loss of a sense of outwardly directed life and death urgency.

The way the core team responds to individuals who are barriers is important. One pastor who was clear and intentional in his approach, was faced with an influential member who clearly resisted the shifts in the church. The individual was unable to accept the outward focus that welcomed a much younger generation of single adults. Particularly troubling was the shift in the worship style, even though it fulfilled the widely owned vision. Aware that the individual had been unable to make the shift from an inward focus to an outward focus, the pastor continually invited the person into transformation in his own life. He was encouraged to embrace the church's focus on the life and death issues for persons being reached by the church. But most importantly, the pastor did not abandon him or discard him. He did, however, make it clear that he would not allow the person to pull the church away from God's call.

Responding to the basic needs of people removes much of their resistance to change. People need to be reminded of the purpose for the change, and some need more help in seeing and understanding the vision than others. Gentle reminders invite the person to understand and embrace the vision. Or a person may need help in seeing how living into the vision is actually possible. The resistance may be based on a genuine fear of failure for the church. The person may need help in seeing how, through the redevelopment journey, the church can actually reach a new place of health and vitality.

Everyone Needs a Place

But most importantly, people need a sense that there is a place for them in the new church that is emerging. Often, resistant people are simply feeling discarded. Having given their lives in significant ways to the church, they see the church moving in directions that no longer value them. An effective and responsible core team sees and affirms the value of longtime faithful workers. The core team understands the importance of the resources that all people bring to the redevelopment journey. The loss of any individual sets the church back. The caring and creativity of the core team ensures an important place for everyone.[3]

Change, however, always brings conflict. Already appearing at previous places on the journey, conflict once again becomes evident as new people are empowered for action and barriers are removed. When conflict is present, a continual focus on the vision is crucial, and the focus remains on what God is calling the church to be. Rather than the change being in response to the desires of individuals, the change serves a compelling mission. God is calling the congregation to cross the line from wishful thinking into action. Now is the time to do what it takes to make sure there are plenty of laborers for the plentiful harvest.

Reflections of a Companion

The sense of urgency was growing. A core team provided stability. The vision was sharpening and taking root in people's hearts. We had prepared the ground and talked about things long enough; people ached to start doing things.

"We have talked a lot about valuing children and young families," Sarah began her phone call. "I know two families with young children who are looking for a church. They want a worship service where their children can be with them for part of the time—but not all of it. It goes fine until sermon time, but then the kids get restless and their parents get anxious. They end up leaving worship tired and frustrated. I bet they are not the only ones. What if I took your sermon theme for the day and created a way to get that idea across to children? I would like to do it and I bet there are some others who might help me."

The clearer and more compelling our vision became, the more individuals seemed to connect their personal and unique passions with the needs around us. It became a normal thing to have someone sidle up to me. "Wouldn't it be great if . . ." they would begin. The more they would talk, the more excited they would get. The picture was so clear for them that I could see it too. What an exciting time, watching people stand up and step out and try new things for our church

It might be considered business as usual for another church in a different community to begin a youth-run coffeehouse showcasing the music, art, and poetry of the youth in the community. But for us, that was way off the charts.

From Dream to Reality

In this stage of redevelopment, we began moving from the realm of dreaming into the land of action. Dreams started materializing as concrete goals. The organizational structure of our church supported this action. In the years before I had arrived, the church had restructured in an attempt to recapture its vitality. The restructuring created a good deal of chaos, without impacting overall church health. It had, however, significantly reduced the amount of permission a person needed to obtain before engaging in ministry. If a ministry fit the vision of the church and the resources were there to support it, the pastor or the committee that oversaw that area of church life could authorize it. The tiers of boards needing to give official nods of approval were gone. Now that we had a vision, the structure worked.

Even though the structure supported turning ideas into reality, it did not always happen. Not everybody with a great idea had the wherewithal to carry it out. Sometimes people tried things that simply did not fly. They possessed great ideas, but did not know how to implement them. Or they knew how to implement them, but ran out of energy. Some did not know who or how to connect with the human and other resources required to sustain it. Sometimes the idea was good, but the form it took simply did not work.

Equipping People for Ministry

These new leaders required help. Simply blessing them and sending them on their way was not enough; in fact, it set them up for failure. At least in the beginning stages of their work they needed guidance and support and in differing amounts depending on their levels of competence and confidence.

Alicia was adamant that every child in our neighborhood have a safe place to go after school where there was a caring adult. She was motivated and determined and did not have a clue how to organize such a thing. Alicia was confident, but not competent—at least not yet. She needed a great deal of direction and training. Our youth staff person stayed right by her side, encouraging her and helping her learn those skills. The more her skills developed, the less direction he provided, until a year later she was not only running things on her own, she was training others.

At the other extreme, Rachel felt compelled to start a group for mothers of preschoolers in the community. She knew exactly what to do and how to do it. Within two weeks of the go-ahead from the church council, she had gathered a steering committee, signed them up for a training seminar that was coming to a nearby city, and developed a basic action plan for the next six months. Rachel did not need direction, just encouragement and some linkage to other interested people and groups in the church.

Excited, challenged, exhausted, and stretched—all those words describe what it was like to provide leadership during that phase. So much was going on all at once. Everywhere you turned, new things were being birthed. Each person, each budding ministry required a different kind of support.

I have to admit, more often than not, when a new effort failed, it was because of a lack of appropriate leadership on my part. My preferred style is to provide support, not direction. I naturally gravitate towards motivating and encouraging, and naturally shy away from giving directions and telling people how to do things. Sometimes, however, specific direction about how to do something was really what was needed. We were a small to midsize church operating in a pastor-centered mode, where the pastor is the central coordinator of church life.[4] Most of the day-to-day support of leaders came from me.

Sometimes I supported them brilliantly; other times I failed miserably. If I could go back in time and do it all over again, I would share that role. I would deputize or consecrate or whatever it took to have the congregation accept someone partnering with me in equipping and supporting leaders.

I would look for someone who loved training and directing motivated people. So many things were emerging all at the same time, I could not and did not provide all that was needed for each person to flourish and grow. Few leaders can provide all the different kinds of support that are needed. Know what you are good at and recruit others to help you in the areas where you are weak.

Running Interference

Empowering people for action defines this stage of the redevelopment process. The difficulty of empowering people became clear as I awakened to the fact that empowering some people might mean disempowering others. I loved creating the environment in which people could bloom. But creating it was not enough; I had to protect it as well. That often meant running interference for these new ministries, helping the leaders identify the blocks and sidestep the dangers.

In inviting people to stretch and dream and try new things, the leadership of the church was encouraging them to do things they had never done before, things they might well fail at several times before ultimately succeeding. That is a vulnerable place to be, made even more tenuous by the response their new thing might evoke. Systems theory tells us that when systems encounter change, the system will naturally and unconsciously resist it and attempt to revert to the way things were. New ministries and the people who started them were natural targets for such resistance.

We encountered little overt opposition. People had such a hand in the discernment of the vision, that by this point, they pretty openly affirmed the direction in which we were moving. Those who took extreme issue with it had left. The blocks and barriers that arose to meet the innovations were much subtler and came in much-loved and well-meaning human form.

The "yeses" we said to the innovators, required us to say some "nos" to those who were invested in keeping things the same. I remember a very tearful meeting with an 80-plus-year-old woman who had served for many years as a committee chair, and had resigned her position earlier that year. She declared it was time for her to move on and she wanted a new generation to carry on the work. Her work on that committee had been her life and she still cared deeply, and it delighted her that others were beginning to feel something of that call; however, she was ready to pass the reigns.

Our church uses a nominating committee to identify and recruit leadership for the various committees and teams. Our nominating committee understood the dynamics of our redevelopment process. Learning of this opening, they recruited a couple that possessed a personal sense of God's urgency, who embodied the vision, and who had both the skills and the motivation to lead that ministry area. They set to work building a new team and setting specific and achievable goals.

Four months following her resignation, the former chair came to see me, wanting her job back. She had been phoning the new chairs weekly to pass along resources and wisdom: she was concerned about their lack of experience, their style of leadership, and the direction the team was moving. Worried about the future of the church, she offered to take back the role of chair. "Maybe a year from now, after I've worked with them for a year, I could retire," she added.

I had talked just the day before with the new chairs. Their vision aligned perfectly with the church's and they were creating exactly what the nominating committee had hoped for. But these new leaders felt frustrated and judged by their predecessor's attempts to be helpful. They wondered if perhaps they were wrong for the job and should resign. I had reaffirmed the particular gifts they brought and reassured them that the nominating committee had selected them for those very gifts. I began to see that if I did not run interference with the former chair and convince her to let go, they would not continue.

The woman showed up in my office while I was dialing her number. "It's not working," she said. "I need to take it back." We talked about how passionately she cared, about how her fear that the church's focus on mission would be lost, about her hopes for the church . . . and mine. We came to understand that we both wanted the same thing and were prepared to do whatever it took for the church to reach that place. It was a holy moment. In that atmosphere of open sharing and deep listening, I told her that I believed her initial instinct was right and that she needed to let go of the committee. The new generation needed to stretch their wings and learn, just as she had. They needed to make their own mistakes along the way and grow from them, just as she had. They were the ones who could help us find our way into this new future, and she agreed. And then, with my heart in my mouth and tears in my eyes, I asked her to let go and step away from the committee for the next year to focus on her own next call.

Tears streaming down her face, she agreed. It was hard for both of us. We cried together at the pain of the saying good-bye to the end of an era. It was one of the hardest things I have done as a pastor, yet strangely enough, it is one of the moments that I am proudest of. I did what it took to protect the new emerging life.

And the woman? She let go of that committee, but not of her passion. Free of the responsibilities of leading a committee, she found new outlets and projects that helped our church continue to grow in vital ministry. She is a marvel.

A People Shaped by the Journey

The core team and I often talked over instances such as the former chair of the committee. We wanted to make sure we did not label people who were having a difficult time changing or who challenged the vision at particular points as being difficult people. Conflict was a learning place. It meant that two or more good ideas were present and that everybody could grow, if we opened ourselves to it. It helped that our meetings were venues where we learned about and discussed change theories. That helped us look at things objectively and remind ourselves that these occurrences were normal and expected and even a sign that we were moving someplace new. Our vision was not to be a church of us versus them. So we had to be careful not to allow ourselves to think in those terms, even in those kinds of challenging moments.

The congregation's new DNA was being shaped by the way we were being, and on the way to where we were going. We might not be in that distant place yet, but we could behave with each other as if we were. Our running joke was that it took Moses and the Hebrew people 40 years to get to the promised land because that is how long it took to make them fit to live there. It certainly was true for me.

The Danger Zone

During that phase of redevelopment, my time was pulled in many directions. On top of all the new and emerging places that called for attention, people still died, got sick, and had life crises. Previously existing programs and committees still demanded my time. Items got added to my schedule, but nothing got taken off. Every yes meant a no to something else. In order to say yes to all those things, I found myself saying no to my personal time. I began to lose my feeling of centeredness.

My evening meditation was the first to go, followed quickly by my morning centering time. It was around that time when I began craving a job where I could have a weekend. Two days off in a row seemed like heaven to me. Flipping burgers, I thought, now that would not be so bad. Do the job and then leave it when you are done. My desire to be the best pastor I could be for the church had led me to ignore the very things that helped me be of value there. I lost my sense of centeredness and groundedness. The work that had always felt like play had lost its fun—it felt like work. And work seemed endless and overwhelming in the energy it demanded. The more I gave, the more it took.

For several months I lived in an increasingly tired and stretched place. Pleased with what the church was experiencing, I nonetheless felt inadequate to juggle all of the responsibilities of leadership. Life in the church often felt like a pressure cooker, and I took on the responsibility to see that things would cook in that environment rather than blow up.

I was one of the leaders at a convocation on redevelopment during that time. For the first time, I heard other presenters share that they had gone through a similar period of overwhelming stress in the midst of their fourth year of redevelopment. What had worked for them? Turning to God. Funny, I had not thought of that.

The next day I surrendered. Kneeling did not seem enough, so I stretched out spread-eagle on the hotel-room floor face down and started talking to God. "I give up! This is too hard. I don't know what to do or how to do it. And I'm so tired I don't care anymore." That was the moment I gave up being the one who was responsible for the change. Staring at the orange shag forest stretching before my eyes, it dawned on me that it wasn't me who would empower these people, but God. I don't know exactly what changed that afternoon, but something did. It wasn't long before I realized that if I wanted a weekend now and then, all I had to do was arrange my schedule that way. And I did. And it works. And I can't believe I didn't do it sooner. Could it be that empowering other people starts with empowering myself?

If you have reached this step in redevelopment, then you have been at this for quite a while now. How is it with your soul? As you begin the work of empowering people for the ministries to which they are called, remember to empower yourself. Connect and root yourself daily in the God from whom all power flows.

Guidance from a Coach

As your vision continues to be owned by an ever-increasing base of people, a new sense of urgency may seem to be emerging. The desire to push forward in creating and carrying out more aspects of the future vision will grip people. More and more people will want to bring a piece of that vision into reality. They are being drawn to it by its compelling nature. So how do they become empowered to do so? How are they equipped to live out the ministry God is calling them to?

Reflect and Journal

The goal for this coaching section is for the core team to develop strategies for the empowerment of people in living out God's vision for your church, to include the removal of barriers to that empowerment. In preparing to work on this goal, it will be helpful to reflect on the current degree of empowerment of the people in your church, and the barriers they may encounter:

- Note the present values and attitudes among the leaders regarding the empowerment of others. Initiate discussions with leaders to explore their values regarding the empowerment of people. Note your feelings about moving into this phase.

- Consider your own level of empowerment as a leader in the church. What are the sources of your empowerment? Consider your own level of empowerment in your personal life. Again, what are its sources?

- What are the current methods or processes by which people are empowered in your church? (Examples: formal nominating process, informal recruitment, casual conversation, spontaneous offers to serve, opportunities to explore individual gifts and skills, skill-training opportunities, systems for mentoring, etc.) How would you describe their effectiveness? Who initiates these methods or processes?

- Where are you observing or hearing reports of barriers to empowerment? (Examples: in the structure; policies; processes; inadequate skills or information; lack of clarity about gifts and strengths; people who are blocking forward motion; lack of effective communication between groups, systems, or individuals; etc.)

- List other ideas to consider the current degree of empowerment of the people.

Develop a Plan

Review the suggested plan to help achieve the goal of empowering people and removing barriers:

- Given the reflection done on the items above, list all the places in the church structure—the policies and the processes—that need adjusting to allow them to promote empowerment, rather then blocking it.

- Prioritize the list to identify the top three or four items that need addressing first.

- Develop a specific action plan to address each of the top items over the next three months.

- After three months, review the progress made, update the original list, prioritize the list, and identify three or four more items to be addressed over an additional time of three months. (Some of these may still be the same items that need more work.) You can see that this will be an ongoing process in the life of your church.

- Develop strategies to encourage and assist people in discovering their passions and gifts for ministry. (See the resource list provided at the end of this book.)

- Develop a plan for mentoring new leaders and providing the support and training they may need.

- Develop a plan to assess and facilitate needed skill training. This would include appropriate training for leaders and volunteers in a variety of roles, from committee members and Sunday school teachers to mission project leaders and church food-bank volunteers.

- Discuss how the core team will deal with individuals who are acting as barriers, always keeping in mind that they are children of God and a part of God's vision. It will be helpful to invite a professional person to assist the group in developing some role-playing exercises to explore various responses to individuals who are acting as barriers. (For further assistance, review the mentor and companion stories in this chapter about people acting as barriers.)

- Develop a plan to address needed improvements in communication patterns, if not already covered in the first item of this list.

- Consider ways to strengthen your own empowerment, both as a church leader and in your personal life.

- List other options for empowering people and removing the barriers.

Chart a Course

Now, determine what you will actually do to empower people and eliminate the barriers to their effective ministry. Review the suggested plan above and identify the specific steps you will take. Be sure your plans are clear and include time frames. Consider which option will be the hardest or most challenging for you to do. How will you ensure that this one gets addressed?

Looking Ahead

As people engage in ministries that reflect their passions and the vision God has for them, it will feel like some things have clicked into place. Vision and action will seem to be meshing and creating the sense of fulfillment that God has in mind for people. Be watching for those moments, no matter how small, so that as the leaders of the church you can identify these directions and actions as being consistent with the vision. It is your job to help people begin to name and celebrate these victories along the way, to praise God for gifting you with this progress. We will explore how to do this in our next session.

NOTES

1.   Christian A. Schwartz, *Natural Church Development* (Carol Stream, Ill.: Church Smart Resources, 1996). *Natural Church Development* uses a consultant-based survey system to help churches identify and target areas that may be limiting growth.

2.   Kenneth Blanchard, Drea Zigarmi, and Patricia Zigarmi, *Leadership and the One Minute Manager* (New York: William Morrow & Company, 1985). Their model offers a method for assessing the most helpful leadership style to use as you relate to persons with differing levels of skill and commitment.

3.   William Bridges, *Managing Transitions* (Reading, Mass.: Addison-Wesley Publishing Company, 1991), 50–66, discusses the need of people to understand the purpose and plan in a change process. Also, he lifts up the importance of people seeing a place for themselves in what is being created.

4.   Appendix D in *Discerning Your Congregation's Future* offers an excellent, concise discussion of congregational size theory. If redevelopment leads your congregation to a size transition, Beth Gaede, editor, *Size Transitions* (Bethesda, Md.: The Alban Institute, 2001) offers a number of helpful articles.

6

Seeing and Celebrating the Foretaste

Observations from a Mentor

The years required to reach this point in the redevelopment process varies from church to church. To address each part of the process in a deliberate, deep, and faithful way takes time. To fail to adequately address some part of the process results in hitting a wall. And there is no way beyond that wall until you go back and address what you skipped over lightly.

Changes Become Visible

More results begin to be seen at this stage of the journey. People experience increased enthusiasm and hope as they sense that something new is emerging. People engage in conversations that reveal more energy and optimism about the future. The focus shifts from concern around survival to an eagerness for the future.

Beyond the change in morale and attitudes, observable results begin to emerge. Often they go unnoticed, but it is important to name them and to celebrate them. Human nature needs to be aware of and see the results of committed work. People eventually begin to ask if what they do makes any difference. Many have been through renewal and revitalization efforts in churches before and some have seen those efforts result in nothing more than temporary hype. Is this just another one of those efforts or are there some concrete results?

A Focus on Results Related to the Vision

What are the appropriate and important results to name and celebrate? The shift in attitudes and morale is important, and naming the shift brings support for the journey. Some may enjoy the improved feelings and think the work is over, the goal accomplished; others will press for specific, statistical data showing that change has happened.

Worship attendance, financial giving, or improvements in the building often become the focus. Attendance and finances are important indicators but can also deceive. Increased attendance may result from a variety of factors that have nothing to do with movement into the vision. An attendance campaign or a dynamic preacher may temporarily increase numbers. An arm-twisting financial drive or a wealthy new participant may boast the financial picture. A bequest could provide a face-lift for the building.

A shift in the mood and improvements in statistics are welcomed and appreciated, but these results may not be indications of living into the vision. On this part of the journey, celebrations need to focus on specific ways in which the vision is embodied in the present life of the church. What is lifted up and celebrated depends on the vision.

If the vision included extending the inclusiveness of the church, look for new persons of differing ethnicity, race, economic status, and lifestyle. Who do you see welcomed and also brought into the core leadership of the church? Identify how the lives of newer people have been enriched. Remember, too, to lift up the ways the church has been enriched by the gifts they bring.

With a vision focusing on lives being changed, look for concrete stories. Where do you see new hope replacing quiet desperation, sobriety replacing addiction, passion for social justice replacing apathy? Tell stories of the transformation of people who had been living without hope. Tell stories of longtime Christians who have had new epiphanies and life-changing experiences. Include stories of people of all ages.

If the vision values caring relationships, where are new, supportive friendships seen? With a vision focusing on caring and service, tell stories of individuals giving themselves to make a difference. Celebrate the mission trip of a group or an individual.

A Foretaste Rather than an Accomplishment

Churches are used to celebrating victories, lifting up results. Churches do experience reasons to rejoice: ending the year with all bills paid, simply surviving for another year, completing a building project, having a record Easter attendance, receiving recognition at the denominational annual meeting—all of these are good reasons to rejoice.

But what is celebrated on this part of the redevelopment journey is different, and the reason for celebrating is different. Celebration often places the center of concern on the life and death of the church, an inward focus. Celebration integral to redevelopment has an outward focus. The rejoicing still lifts up issues of life and death, but it is the life and death of people, not of the institution.

A foretaste of the future is what is being celebrated. What is lifted up encourages and inspires people, creating a desire for more of the good results. Each celebration is not a conclusion, an ending; instead, each celebration prepares people to better recognize and welcome more of the fruits God has in mind for the church. The rejoicing is a momentary pause to notice what God is doing and to give thanks. The victory becomes a confirmation of what is possible.

Celebrating through Storytelling

Stories are central to celebration—they focus on what is happening in the lives of people and in relationships. The story of an individual who experiences personal transformation is powerful. These stories are so important in the redevelopment process. By this point in the redevelopment process, stories abound yet they often go unheard. A dramatic, quick change in a person's life makes an impact. But gradual changes happening over time, even though just as significant, go unnoticed. All those stories of new life for individuals are reminders of what God is doing in our midst.

One church, a predominately Anglo church in a changing neighborhood, saw and celebrated living into their vision. A single Hispanic mother joined the church one Sunday morning. An elderly Anglo woman, a long-time member of the church, stood with her as her sponsor. She could have just been another new member, but the pastor and other leaders in the church were able to see more. No goal had been set to bring new Hispanic members in, but the church had identified connecting with the diverse population in their neighborhood in deep and caring ways as part of their vision and values. Here was evidence.

Curiosity led the pastor to talk more with the elderly woman who was the sponsor. In their conversation, he learned of the change in her life during the last several years. He heard about her movement from resentment of the new Hispanic population group in the neighborhood to a curiosity and then a concern for them. Relating to this single mother was a way she opened herself up to change in her own life. And what a powerful story this was as it was told with respect and reverence at the church's monthly council meeting.

Another church, midway in the redevelopment journey, celebrates victories every Sunday. In worship the church visibly lives out its vision of weaving together the neighborhood, living out God's command to love thy neighbor. People of diverse ages and races from the neighborhood join with the older Anglos as leaders in worship. Among the leaders are residents from the group recovery house located close to the church.

With the vision of every member being in ministry, another church celebrates the ways in which individuals take responsibility to combine their passions with service. One woman followed her passion and initiated a monthly opportunity for English-speaking and Spanish-speaking children and parents to come together. The opportunity helps each group to become increasingly bilingual as well as develop cross-cultural awareness. The church celebrates the ministry but they most especially celebrate that woman living out her passion.

Now is the time for the entire church to become alert to stories. Even though the stories may be happening all around, it takes some practice to see them. Name for yourself the key elements of the vision and then identify the behaviors and events that will indicate growth in those areas. Where do you need to be looking? Power and energy build as a church begins to see and experience a foretaste of the future.

How to Use Stories

And how do you use these stories? Some stories are simply to be pondered by the person seeing or hearing them. Others are talked about with another core team member. Certain stories might be used to encourage another person, while others are appropriate in more public settings—council meetings, even public worship. And some need to be told as first person testimonies of the transforming presence of God. The core team actively looks for the stories and guides how to use them. But beware of using the stories as a weapon. Beware of using them as a "thou should" to someone. Stories are neither weapons nor gossip. Stories are always told to let people know what is possible. They invite the other person to reflect on the unique way in which God may be nudging her.

And just as telling a story is a gift to another person, listening to a story is also a gift. A good listener helps a person find his story. The listener nudges a person to explore his story, seeing meanings beyond the surface. The person can become more open to the even greater stories God wants to live out in his life.

Measuring Progress

The question of whether the work has made a difference is asked in many ways, but seldom is an answer given: "How do we measure progress? How do we know if we are actually going someplace? Are we just spinning our wheels? Are we just kidding ourselves?" Well, how do you know?

Traditional statistics are important indicators, but traditional statistics are also heavily influenced by situations. If your goal is to live into the vision that God has given to you, what better way to gather data for evaluation than to listen to stories. Are there stories of lives being transformed? Are people living by new norms, giving priority to the people and the values lifted up in the vision? Do you see specific parts of the vision being lived out in new ways through the behavior of people? The core team monitors movement on the redevelopment journey. If the fruits are not present, if the foretaste is not experienced, then leaders know that a part of the redevelopment process needs to be revisited in order to move forward.

Enjoy reaching the place where stories emerge for people to hear and rejoice over. Use the stories for encouragement. Celebrate the goodness of God and give thanks for the commitment and faithfulness of people. Take a deep breath and move forward into the even greater things God is eager to give.

Reflections from a Companion

Redevelopment is hard work. After investing so much heart and soul and energy, Valley View Church really needed to know if it was making any difference. The biggest question the church faced in that regard was figuring out what to measure.

Early after my arrival, attendance and giving went up. I charted those indicators very carefully, so I know. That is what I had been trained to keep track of. The formula was clear. Increased worship attendance plus increased financial giving equals increased vitality. But did it really? Looking back at the attendance records for the past 30 years raised some questions about that generally accepted formula.

Charted, our attendance figures revealed a regular series of gently rounded peaks and troughs. Attendance would reach a certain high point and then automatically begin to head downward until a certain low point seemed to trigger an upward swing. Up and down, up and down. For the past 15 years, however, the regular peaks and troughs had consistently followed a downward trend until the bottom had seemingly dropped out shortly before my arrival. The chart's neat pattern of waves ended with a continuous downward line.

The last three years, however, saw the line measuring worship attendance climbing upward. Increases in attendance energized the church. People liked seeing the sanctuary fuller, but were we changing? Or were we simply returning to the same old pattern? And what did that pattern mean? Increased worship attendance by itself did not necessarily indicate a fundamental shift in the DNA of the church. I could easily imagine a jazzy marketing plan temporarily swelling the numbers beyond where they had been without anything essential changing.

Deciding What to Measure

If we celebrated "bigness," we wondered among ourselves at a core team meeting one night, wouldn't that indicate that "big" was what we valued? Yet, "big" hadn't shown up as a value as we had envisioned and still was not of critical importance to us. We had limited resources of time, energy, and space in our communication vehicles (newsletter, bulletin boards, conversations, etc.). If we used those resources to spotlight how big we were getting, what would we be ignoring? What might get lost in the shadows? We did not want to spend our resources highlighting and celebrating things of lesser importance. We wanted to invest our limited resources for maximum effect. Lifting something up and saying, "Wow, look at this. Isn't this great!" focuses attention in a particular direction and draws energy to it. Celebration magnifies the event being celebrated.

The discussion deepened. What did we value? And how could we celebrate that value when we saw flashes of it in our midst? We had to look first at our future vision, and then at our current reality, and then point at the things happening now that we believed foreshadowed the future.

In old horror movies, you can always tell from the music when the monster is about to appear—the music foreshadows his arrival. We listened for the same kind of thing, but only in a good way. We searched for the foreshadowing of the "kin-dom" of God. We still tracked all the traditional kinds of indicators: membership, attendance, and giving. The church shared that information freely, but in a low-key way. We reserved our hoopla for the visible evidence of those goals, and ways of being which the church said it valued most deeply.

We valued diversity, so we began looking for signs of it. That was fairly simple. We could look at the ages of the people that were joining us, and the ethnicities, the sexual orientations, and the variety of economic levels. Increases in variety in any of those categories indicated that we were moving towards our vision. That was something to celebrate.

Ways of Celebrating

And how would we celebrate? It depended on the situation. The first time an infant was part of worship and began to cry, we simply stopped and gave thanks for that sound and that life. That alerted people to the fact that we had a baby with us. It framed a crying child as something worthy of thanks.

The first person wearing a nose ring in worship warranted a story at that next week's committee meetings. I invested my airtime in those settings in pointing out that a young adult found our church to be life giving to her, a place where she connected with God and her best self. We were already becoming what we longed to be, and I championed that.

Newsletter articles, sermon illustrations, discussions and reports during committee meetings, one-on-one conversations—all were vehicles for pointing out and celebrating the emerging vision. One Easter, we even created a bulletin board that invited people to post photos and articles that revealed what God was birthing in us. People themselves then took responsibility for looking for signs of life. It forced them to think about our vision and values and come up with a concrete symbol of it. When the vision and values came out of our mouths and hands, they held more meaning for us.

Recognizing the Signs of New Life

For us, change generally happened so slowly and gradually that people needed help in seeing the shifts. Sometimes it was discomfort that first focused someone's attention on how something had changed. "I could not see past that tall young stranger who sat in front of me this morning." "There was a child in back of me that kicked my pew all through the service." Those comments initially carried negative emotion. The core team, staff, and I had to help people view those same experiences from a different perspective. There were young adults in our midst . . . and children . . . exactly what we had envisioned. As long as those things truly could be seen as concrete manifestations of the vision, people seemed able to make the mental shifts it took to welcome them. Celebrating such things was certainly a change.

When we began the redevelopment process, the church naturally rejoiced when an end-of-the-year appeal brought in enough money to cover the bills. Jubilation prevailed when a planned "Miracle Sunday" raised the needed funds to replace the roof. The church excelled at celebrating those kinds of things—the fixing of problems, the survival of another year.

We needed to stop celebrating survival and learn how to celebrate the movement of the Spirit, the transformation of lives, and the giving of self to transform the world. Even though we had reclaimed a mission of transformation as our reason for being, it had been so long since the church had lived that out, that they were not really sure what missional living looked like or how it felt. Our first reaction to signs of new life was often confusion rather than excitement.

Often the little wins seemed as much a threat as a victory. The youth minister shared with the church council the changes he was seeing in a troubled youth who had become part of the church. Some nodded approvingly during the telling, while others shook their heads about having "those kinds of kids" in the church.

We learned that a "win" was not necessarily something that made us feel warm and comfy. A "win" was something that indicated we were moving towards our vision—something that was a foretaste of the future.

Storytelling as Celebration

We encouraged people to observe what was going on in our midst and to tell those stories. Stories present events from a particular perspective and thus make meaning of those occurrences. Our perspective was grounded in the assumption that God was actively doing something in our midst. As events happened, that perspective was the lens we looked through to make sense of them. We began to develop stories about what God was doing in our midst.

We told the stories of the individuals through whom we saw God working. Another of our values was empowering service, so we lifted up the story of Tom. His work with the local food bank alerted him to the conditions of a large group of migrant workers camped on a riverbank as they waited for the weather to allow work to begin. The tiny community where the workers were camped had no resources and little desire to help them. He arranged for a local store to donate sleeping bags, pulled together some folks from the church, filled the church van with the bags and food, and headed out. Tom and his crew were the compassionate and caring hands of God. Some might be tempted to view that as a one-time isolated event, but when reports of multiple such events began drifting back, it became clear that something fundamental was shifting.

The church celebrated the story of Stacy. Her love for teenagers and passion for peace led her to volunteer at a church camp for youth in Macedonia where youth from the conflicting religious and political factions (Serbians, Croatians, and ethnic Albanians) came together to build connections for peace. She was the first missionary our church had commissioned and sent in over a decade. She talked about hearing God's call in a way that led a whole new generation in our church to wonder how they were called to be a part of God's work in the world.

A Growing Edge

The biggest stretch for us was celebrating personal transformation. Not because we did not value it, but because we were not used to talking about it. Our church culture shied away from sharing things of a deeply personal nature. Traditionally, personal concerns shared during prayer time rarely moved beyond a surface level. It was not uncommon for marriages to fall apart, for families to enter bankruptcy, or for children to enter rehabilitation programs without the church community ever knowing about it until it was over.

It was the newcomers and the youth who led the way for us. Unaware of the norms and unwritten rules, they shared their hearts and let people see into their lives. By that time, we had talked enough about the culture we wanted that when those things were shared, they were received as holy offerings. We heard Sunday by Sunday of David's struggle to stay sober. We accompanied Jill through her struggle with breast cancer, by having a different person meeting her at the hospital each day to support and pray for her during her radiation treatments, which helped to ease her fears. Those stories testified to God's action in real lives right in our midst.

In some other church, these might be normal, run-of-the mill things. But for us, they were radical shifts from the ways life together and ministry had been. They were signs that new life was rooting and growing in us and beginning to bear fruit. If you are at this point in the process of redevelopment, what are the radical shifts that are taking place in your church? What fruit is your work bearing?

Celebrating those little victories created momentum. Small by themselves, linked together these little short-term wins gave all of us hope and energy. They helped us see that we really were making progress on our journey. And they helped us learn to better recognize the promised land towards which we were heading. Celebrating the right things was not just fun or energizing, it was an essential part of becoming the vision we beheld.

What are the signs of new life in your congregation? As you work with the coach across the next months in searching for and celebrating those signs of life, remember to give thanks to the God who brings them.

Guidance from a Coach

In the previous coaching section, the focus was on empowering people and removing the blocks that might keep them from living into the vision God has in mind for them. At this point in the redevelopment process, as the core team gathers, more stories are being shared about concrete ways in which the vision is being realized. You may hear more narratives about ways in which people's faith lives are being transformed. Hallelujah! Utilize and build on this by intentionally naming and celebrating these moments of living into the vision.

Celebrating small steps along the way can further build momentum. Just as a compelling vision initially draws people to it, now the realization that it is actually becoming reality can be further motivation to faithfully move forward. It can further inspire a group to continue on its chosen path towards the vision. Naming and celebrating results can also help to clarify and fine-tune the vision itself. In a sense, it can help the core team test the vision in real-life conditions, and make needed adjustments in either the vision or the major strategies for fulfilling it.

Be aware that while naming and celebrating a step in living out the vision may create renewed momentum for some people, the same step may create great fear, defensiveness, or anxiety in others. Both the mentor and companion sections describe situations in which people are stretched out of their comfort zones by progress being made to realize the vision. Leaders and the core team will want to strategize some ways to help people process these reactions.

Reflect and Journal

The goal for this coaching section is for the core team to develop strategies to name and celebrate the moments of living into the vision. To prepare yourselves to develop these strategies, reflect on the following questions and record your responses in your journal.

- What are you observing and sensing from others that points to evidence of the vision coming to fruition?

- What are you hearing from others that points to evidence of the vision being realized?

- Where has celebrating already taken place that you know of? (Examples: stories told; people being encouraged to continue with behavior that supports the vision; special focus at meetings, in worship, in printed communications that highlight examples of the vision being realized; etc.)

- Where have you been most stretched and uncomfortable thus far? What has given you the most cause for celebration?

- Given the feedback, is God calling you to adjust the vision in any way?

- List other questions to help you reflect on this goal.

Develop a Plan

Next, review the following suggested plan for developing strategies to name and celebrate the short-term wins in living into the vision.

- Discuss what it is you are looking for in stories that might be lifted up for celebration. As outlined in the mentor section, things to celebrate might include behaviors, fruits in the lives of people, energy that becomes present, optimism about the future, shifts in attitudes, and so forth. How do you know when the vision is being realized in your setting?

- Discuss the appropriate use of stories. Brainstorm the various ways in which stories might be used, depending on the circumstances of the story. (Review the helpful description of the use of stories, found near the end of the mentor section and throughout the companion section.)

- Develop a plan for collecting and sharing (celebrating) stories. Name the various methods for becoming aware of stories. Create a time line to ensure the regular sharing and celebrating of the stories.

- Discuss the need to watch for spontaneous moments when it is critical for someone to identify a short-term win right on the spot. Agree together to stretch yourselves to do this, sharing with each other and celebrating when various opportunities have been utilized. Record these moments in your journal. After three months, note potential settings that may be underutilized for this purpose. Challenge yourselves to make better use of these settings for celebrating the vision coming to fruition.

• Discuss how you will assist people in processing the fears and anxieties that can be created by the movement towards God's vision. How will you create time and space for this kind of processing? What questions might you ask? How will you demonstrate respect for their feelings and concerns, even if you do not share similar feelings? What encouragement will you offer?

• Discuss the ways in which you might assist people in celebrating the very personal matters of spiritual growth and personal transformation.

• List other options to achieve your goal.

Chart a Course

In reviewing the suggested plan above, consider which ones are the most helpful for your setting. Decide what you will do to develop strategies to name and celebrate the short-term wins in realizing the vision. Write down the steps you will take as clearly as possible and, when applicable, the time frame you will be working within. And enjoy the celebrating to the glory of God.

Looking Ahead

It could be tempting to let the redevelopment process stall with the celebration of a few short-term wins. Victory could be declared, and everyone could sit back and rest. But if a group is truly desirous of living into the vision God has for it, they must always be on the search for ways in which that vision is evolving. So how do they move forward with redevelopment becoming a way of life? This will be the topic in our next chapter.

7

Building Momentum throughout the Organization

Observations from a Mentor

At this current stage of the redevelopment process, encouraging results have emerged and are routinely celebrated. Short-term victories assure the congregation and the core team that the work has been worth the effort. Temptation can lure you to declare a complete victory at this point. Though improvements are evident, stopping now would leave the church far short of redevelopment. To move on to the place of significant change, the momentum must continue and even build. The changes seen in isolated places must continue until redevelopment permeates all parts of the church.

Lured to Stop, Called to Move Forward

The stage of building momentum is one of the most dangerous in the redevelopment process. Redevelopment efforts often end here. A sense of satisfaction sets in over what has been achieved. People can easily slip into declaring that the church has arrived. They begin settling in and enjoying the good things accomplished.

If crisis has been one of the motivators, the improvement reduces and soon eliminates the urgency. Persons who had great enthusiasm for the redevelopment journey are now ready to enjoy a comfortable circle of friends. The desire to enjoy what has been realized replaces the desire for what is coming.

In many settings, plateaus, especially in worship attendance, appear at this stage of the journey. Frequently the pastor who has been there for five to 10 years will begin to feel that perhaps she has completed her mission in this setting. She experiences appreciation from some people while others slip into complacency. Still others express resistance to any further movement forward into change. Feeling discouragement, the pastor allows herself to slip into feeling she has accomplished the purpose God had in mind for her. But the journey for the church is far from being over. And in many cases, the work God has in mind for the pastor in that setting is far from over.

Periods of extreme effort and concentration have to be balanced with periods of relaxation. Seasons are a normal part of life, and allowing a dormant time renews the person for continued work. Claiming time for rest is crucial, but in even those periods of rest, the deep and holy urgency to move forward remains.

Resistance and Conflict

Introducing change elicits resistance and the strength and determination of the resistance sometimes surprises, even shocks the core team. Sometimes the resistance comes through vocal persons and the sources are clear; at other times, collusion, a silent conspiracy that the people themselves may not even be aware of, is the source.

Resistance to change actually signals strength within the organization. The resiliency providing the resistance keeps the organization from being easily destroyed by negative forces. But the same resiliency makes it difficult for the organization to engage in change, even when that change is positive and health giving. Small changes bringing improvement are welcomed, but a natural preservation reaction is triggered when an organization is on the verge of actually becoming something new and different. What is ultimately life giving is perceived as destructive. Fear of losing something valued activates a defense.

Conflict to some degree is present from the first day commitment is made to congregational redevelopment. People look at the same issues and have different opinions about solutions, and differing opinions bring conflict. Conflict emerges again in a heightened degree as the church celebrates short-term victories. People begin to sense that change may move them beyond their comfort level. With the goal of change permeating all segments of the church, increased conflict develops. The challenge is to learn to use differing opinions in helpful, creative ways rather than pretending the differences do not exist.

Becoming more aware of the differing ways people respond to conflict is helpful. Developing processes that the church agrees on for utilizing conflict in a positive way is crucial. One church asks people to make a covenant to bring their concerns directly to the core team. The core team makes the commitment to seriously respond to each concern, addressing the needs and values of people. Their goal in the midst of conflict is to honor individuals, benefit from their insights, and keep the process moving forward.[1]

Keep the vision at the center of all discussions and decisions. Help people focus on the future into which God is calling the church. Bring them back to the question of what best serves the movement towards that future which God envisions. Focusing on the purpose for redevelopment centers people and directs them to the values held in common.

Revisiting Stages of the Journey

During the redevelopment journey, prior parts of the journey do need to be revisited. Even though the work was done adequately at the time, adjustments or additional work may be needed later. One church found that the core team needed significant reforming. It initially included people who represented two ethnic groups just beginning to be reached by the church. Over a period of several years, those groups had become fully a part of church life and a new immigrant group was starting to move into the neighborhood. In an effort to remain true to their vision, the church began looking for ways to draw someone from this newest group onto the core team. Another church found itself complacently living their once challenging vision. This congregation recognized the need to enlarge their vision so that it could once again draw them forward.

Churches in this stage frequently experience the need to revisit their sense of urgency. A strong outward-focused urgency is essential for continued forward movement. Without that outward-focused urgency, people turn their energy towards maintaining what has been created, and movement forward grinds to a halt. The danger is that at this point in the redevelopment journey, only portions of the church have experienced deep change; the entire church system has not. Yet this is the hump in the transformational process; not because the work is hard, but because it seems easy. A false sense of completion lulls the church into complacency. Revisting and nuturing that sense of holy urgency is critical.

The Regrounding of Leaders

The task of building momentum challenges the core team leaders personally. The team feels great about what is happening as people work together cooperatively. New people are being welcomed. Stories of living into the vision are told and celebrated. All of these accomplishments draw leaders into thankfulness for what has been achieved.

Unexpectedly, a sharp word of criticism comes at the least expected time and sometimes from the least expected place. A group of people in the church reverts to old inward-focused behavior or a decision is made that ignores the vision and values that appeared to be increasingly affirmed.

The core team has been an important community for its members, and now is the time when that supportive community is needed more than ever. The core team members provide each other, and then the church, with support and encouragement as they hold fast to the vision. They revisit the steps of the journey, remembering the ways in which God opened doors at difficult times. Through sharing, scripture, and prayer, individuals are grounded again in what sustains them for the journey. Mistakes are acknowledged. Concerns and hurts of people affected by changes are recognized. Remembering a God-given mission, members of the team renew their commitment. Supported and encouraged by caring relationships with each other, they move forward.

Responding to Additional Barriers

As a part of extending the change throughout the congregational system, barriers have been identified and many removed. Some, however, may still block forward movement. Are there cliques that exist from the past or have more recently formed that are invested in hanging onto something that would be detrimental to movement? What about individuals who may even be highly regarded and who have made positive contributions but who also have a high need for control? What persons and what groups have influence and power and seem to hold hostage the leadership and the redevelopment journey? Are there policies still in place that shut down people and ministries and that are needed to move more fully into the vision? Are there parts of the organizational structure from the past, or even a newly created structure, that is not functional and that does not serve movement into the vision?

Some barriers can be seen. Others are not visible but must still be addressed. Every organization, every church, has norms. Norms are the unwritten rules that guide behavior in a system. The current norms may have served the organization well at one time, but with changes in the environment, these same norms may now inhibit health and vitality. The unspoken expectation that members make their major financial contributions annually in the fall served one church quite well in its agrarian days. Now that a growing suburb encompasses the church, encouraging pledges to be paid weekly or monthly may better serve the church.

At another church, the expectation that children of all ages would sit with parents throughout worship worked for the two parent families that formerly made up the bulk of the congregation. That expectation still exists even though the church serves primarily single-family households whose parents cherish time alone in worship. At this stage of the process, the core team and congregations need to identify the existing norms and determine if they serve the best interests of the vision. New norms may be needed for you to continue moving into a new future.[2]

One of the powerful barriers to a church continuing to move forward is assumptions made about the pastor's role. As a church changes, especially if it changes in size, the way that the pastor relates to the people and to the entire organization also often needs to change. In particular, if a church's vision calls for or results in movement from an average worship attendance of under 150 to over 150, significant challenges face the pastor.[3] Without those shifts, the pastor herself becomes a barrier.

Organizational structures can also block a church's movement forward. A good structure does not in itself bring vitality, but a poor structure can hinder ministry. This is a good time to look at the organizational structure of the church to determine if any changes need to be made to better support the ministries that are emerging. Form should follow function. Structures shift to support the new way in which the church is living out its call.

Assessing and Improving Ministries

Tools to diagnose the strength and effectiveness of ministries are very useful, and the building momentum stage of redevelopment is a good time to use those tools. Depending on tools too heavily in the early stages of redevelopment invites a church to abandon the harder work of redevelopment. Improved worship, an expanded education program, or the adding of a small-group ministry often promises the answer a church wants. When the deeper issues of urgency, vision, and empowerment are not addressed, any quick improvement is only temporary. But the time does come for looking at the individual ministry components, such as worship or education, in the church. For momentum and vitality to continue, all the parts of the system need development in order to serve the vision.

A ministry assessment process allows a church to look at specific ministry areas. Is the church adequately supporting persons in the development of spirituality? Are people guided in discovering their strengths for ministry and then connected with ministry opportunities? Does the church understand and respond to needs of persons outside the church in a relationship building way? A good ministry assessment tool prods a church to examine a wide range of ministry areas. The process gives a church a picture of its strengths and weaknesses. The specific vision of the church influences which areas become a focus for immediate further development.[4]

Momentum builds throughout the organization and change extends to all of the parts. Years of work and commitment bring you to this stage of the process. God calls you to use what God has given you during those years. Use what you have been given and continue to move forward.

Reflections of a Companion

Conflict has gotten a bad rap. Really, your attitude and experience of it all depends on your perspective. Consider conflict as a battle and you will walk into every meeting armed and waiting to be jumped. Think of conflict as a plague to be avoided and you will spend your energy suppressing your thoughts and feelings and living on antacids.

The perspective that church leadership chose to take about conflict became crucial to us in our sixth year. After the storms had blown up around our vision, things had quieted down. Groups and individuals had settled into focused work. Ministry blossomed. The staff and I had just listed 12 new ministries that had not existed a year ago. Energy was good, satisfaction was high, and then, all of sudden, the grumbling started up again. It was different this time, but I had a hard time putting my finger on how it was different. A passing comment about the worship bulletins, an off-hand remark about the tidiness of the building—small things that indicated that people thought things were not quite as they should be. It built slowly until what the staff and I refer to as "the day."

Conflict Revisited

The first of the phone calls came at 9:15 A.M., and by the time I left to go home that afternoon, there were three. Each caller pointed out at great length a different aspect of the church or its programming that was not working the way they thought it should or could. Jack protested about a pledge drive that we were about to undertake. Penny objected to the way a new policy was worded. Alana worried about conflict bubbling between the youth and one of their leaders.

Each long phone call elicited helpful information and ended positively. While I was engaged in the conversations, I could appreciate how important they were. Yet as I drove home that evening, my perspective on the day as a whole was negative. This had been a day of complaints, of conflict met and parried. I am getting pretty good at putting out fires, I thought ruefully. But why all the negative responses right now? Life in the church had been smooth sailing for almost 18 months. As I changed clothes, I worried over whether we were slipping backwards. Even as I thought about it, something within me steeled, preparing to fight for this church I cared so much about.

I had just started stirring the spaghetti sauce when call number four came. With the first words, my chest constricted. Another one. Arghh! But I am so glad that call came. If Henry had not called that evening with concerns about the nursery, I might never have understood the deeper meaning of all those phone calls. While they presented themselves in a manner much like the conflict we had endured before, they were different. In reality, those phone calls heralded the arrival of a whole new phase in our redevelopment process.

"I hate to bother you," Henry began, "but Sue and I feel like we need to say something. It's about the nursery. We read the new brochure about the church. It's great! But . . . it says we offer excellent childcare in our nursery and, well, our experience is that we don't. It's OK, not so bad that we didn't use it, but nowhere near excellent. Olivia moved to the toddler room a couple of weeks ago, so in some ways it's not our concern anymore. As we read that brochure though and thought about the new families that would be coming, we really want it to be excellent for them. We don't want anything to get in their way of experiencing everything this church has to offer them."

A New Perspective

As he talked further, my mind bubbled as fast as the sauce. I suddenly understood what I had missed earlier in the day. Henry was not calling to complain. That was not what this was about at all. Henry and Sue felt personally responsible for the experience of our newcomers. They had caught an inconsistency between what we said and what we did. They felt compelled to help move something from "good enough" to "excellent." Neither Sue nor Henry served in any leadership capacity. They attended most Sundays and had begun in the last year to participate in a few of the ministries.

We chatted a bit longer and decided that a meeting of parents would be the best next step. Together we could brainstorm the elements of excellent childcare. That picture could then guide its creation.

As I was later washing the dishes, I pondered the idea that Henry's phone call had been a sign of his deep investment in the mission and ministry of the church and a signal that he was ready and willing to help take things to the next level. Could it be possible that had been true for each of the calls? As I walked back through the previous phone callls, I could see it clearly. What a different perspective on the day! From that place, the calls were not complaints but declarations of commitment. What if we could honor them as that and help such people form the nucleus of mini-change efforts in their own areas of interest.

There was conflict all right. Our longed for church was popping the seams of its cocoon and starting to emerge. Where before the leadership had pushed and stretched the congregation, now the congregation was pushing and stretching us!

Picking Up Speed

That is when the momentum really began to build. I shudder when I think how close I came to closing the gate on it. The congregation owned the vision. Energized and committed people stood poised and ready to reach out to children and youth, to elderly adults, to diverse populations. The church hummed with their urgency. As exciting as it was, this was a critical point. The teams and committees that had nurtured the change could easily have become barriers to it.

Let us stay with the nursery as an example. The children's ministries team had worked hard over the previous two years crafting programs in response to the needs of the children that were arriving, including nursery service for infants. They could perceive phone calls like Henry's as complaints about what they had created or they might take those phone calls as suggestions for which they as a committee were responsible for acting upon. They chose a different path from either.

Their purpose needed to shift, they decided. Previously this team invented and implemented programs; now, they would focus their energy on empowering others to do that. The team's job would now shift to enlisting, training, and supporting people in creating and implementing children's ministries. That meant that where before only one group developed children's ministries, now we might have six groups that did; for example, nursery, preschool, early elementary, older elementary, the bilingual play group, and the interschool program. More things could happen with more people providing leadership. Coordination by the children's ministries team would ensure that each ministry group would remain connected to the greater vision of the church while receiving resourcing and support.

That change in function necessitated the reconfiguration of the team. It turned out that when the focus shifted, so did the membership. Some people loved the hands-on work with children and program development that had previously been their domain. They shifted to working with one of the ministry sub-teams. Others embraced the idea of being a leader who developed leaders. Training and empowering others emerged as their natural gift.

How often the group met and what they did when they met changed along with their function. They decided all those things themselves, starting with the question, "What's the best way we can enlist, train, and support our leaders in children's ministries?" When they had answered that question, they then decided among themselves what that meant for how often they needed to meet as a group and what they would do with each other when they did.

Realigning the Structure

This phase of our redevelopment journey was marked by attention to our organizational structure. The restructuring that had taken place before my arrival had been functional enough. As significant shifts in our work took place, Valley View's once streamlined structure had adjusted and adapted. At this point the church's organizational chart looked like a house that had undergone multiple remodelings and additions. Ungainly as it was at times, it worked.

In this sixth year, however, it seemed as if ministries emerged almost weekly. More people were connecting with their gifts and strengths and feeling urgency around putting them to good use. New teams were constantly being formed for a specific purpose and then disbanding when their task was over. Those teams did not always receive the direction or support that they needed, thus hindering their work. Valley View needed a good workable organizational structure that could both support the work and adapt to change. The increasing momentum pushed us to find a structure that could both support it and direct it.

The church council decided that form should follow function, so they examined the function of the church. At its simplest, they decided a church invites, incorporates, transforms, and sends. A church invites through personal witness and invitation, effective and congruent marketing, and hospitality to the resulting newcomers. Incorporating people into the life of the church involves adopting newcomers into the family, bringing lapsed members back into connection with the congregation, and developing Christian community. A church supports personal ongoing spiritual transformation through corporate worship and a weekly rhythm of sabbath, small groups for learning, support, accountability, and dialogue, and through instruction in daily personal rituals and disciplines for encountering God. The sending function includes assisting people in identifying their spiritual gifts, ministry within the local church, and ministry to the community and world beyond it.

Our goal was to design a structure that would support those four aspects of our work. Such a structure would not only facilitate ministry, but it would keep us focused on the strategic tasks of the church and insure they were being addressed.

The structure we finally settled on did both. The four major ministry areas each had a two-person team to lead it. Each area was given the authority to form and disband ministry teams in response to the gifts resident in the congregation and the needs present in the community. In addition to the ministry areas and their task teams, four ministry support teams focused on providing the resources the ministry areas needed to do their work. The finance committee developed and administered financial resources, the trustees worked with the physical plant, the staff-parish relations committee focused on the development of a staffing model that supported the ministry of the church, and the nominations committee focused on the identification, development, and support of lay leadership. Representatives from the eight areas met monthly with each other for communication, resourcing, and support, and quarterly with at-large representatives from the church to discuss the strategic direction of the church.

The people in the church who loved order and organization finally began to breathe more easily as a sensible structure came into being. With an effective structure in place, the dreamers could dream, the doers could do, the leaders could lead, and God's vision picked up speed. That structure worked for us at that moment in history. God will lead you in finding the structure that best serves your church.

You and your congregation have nurtured a sense of holy urgency. A powerful and committed group of leaders have helped a compelling vision take root in people's hearts. People are hearing God's call to them and stepping forward to offer themselves in ministry. Your congregation has come so far. Do not stop now. Take a deep breath and let the coach lead you into the next step towards vitality.

Guidance from a Coach

In this stage of the development process, the core team must focus on building momentum throughout the church organization. This momentum is necessary if a church is to continue realizing God's vision for it. This time when successes are so evident is precisely the time that the church will be lured into declaring that all goals have been achieved and that the redevelopment effort is completed.

The mentor and companion sections have outlined the need for the core team to build momentum by addressing several key points:

- continuing to listen for and focus on the vision from God for this church
- dealing with the lure to conclude the redevelopment process

- the grounding and focus of the core team
- responding to additional barriers that block movement toward the vision
- assessing and improving various ministries of the church

Reflect and Journal

The goal for this coaching section is for the core team to develop a plan to build momentum throughout the church organization. In preparing to develop this plan, first assess your current situation by reflecting on the following questions. Record your responses in your journal.

- What temptations to declare victory and sit back to rest are tugging at you currently? How are you dealing with them?

- What similar temptations are you hearing from others in the congregation? Do you have awareness of how people are dealing with them?

- What is the current level of holy urgency in the people of the church? How would you characterize and describe it? Is it the same or different from when you began this process?

- What barriers are currently blocking people from more fully living into the vision? (Review the chapter on empowerment to consider possible barriers.)

- What is the focus of the core team and other major leaders? Include such leaders as chairpersons of boards and other major decision-making groups if they are not part of the core team. Is most energy spent on actions that support realizing the vision in some way?

- List other areas you may wish to reflect on.

Develop a Plan

Next, review the following suggested plan to achieve your goal of developing a plan to build momentum throughout the church organization.

- Discuss how core team members can help each other deal with the various temptations to conclude the redevelopment process. Reflect on the following scripture passages and consider their meaning for your situation: Mark 10:17-22; Luke 18:9-14; Matt. 4:1-11; and Luke 9:28-35. What additional biblical parallels come to mind? How will you support and challenge each other when being lured to stop?

- Strategize various settings in which leaders can initiate honest discussions with other church participants about the temptations to declare the process completed. Discuss appropriate ways to shape and facilitate such gatherings. Also, consider how core team members will respond when such temptations are voiced in informal settings. Practice role-playing such situations.

- Develop a plan for strengthening the sense of holy urgency. Determine the processes and settings you will use for listening to people. (Examples: intentional methods, spontaneous opportunities.) Include plans for listening to new people participating in your church. (Review the methods used in chapter 1 for surfacing the sense of holy urgency.)

- What barriers to empowerment need to be addressed? Prioritize which ones need to be addressed first, and develop a plan to deal with each one. (Review the steps for dealing with barriers in chapter 5.)

- Based on your reflections above, does the focus of the core team and other major leaders need any adjustment? If so, discuss what these adjustments are. How will you shift your focus? When this shift has taken place, how will your behavior be different? How will you encourage church leaders who are not part of the core team to evaluate and make needed adjustments in their focus?

- Could the use of a ministry assessment tool help to focus your work? If so, research which tool(s), and make plans for implementation. (Suggested tools are listed in the list of resources provided in this book.)

- List other options to achieve the goal you have thought of.

Chart a Course

Next, review the suggested plan above and determine what steps you will take to build momentum throughout your church organization. Be as clear and specific as you can be in your plans. Include a time frame whenever possible. What will it take to ensure that each step will be completed, even the one you find most challenging?

Looking Ahead

The momentum that permeates an entire system can, in turn, support and encourage more change. In a healthy church system, that change is driven by a desire to fulfill the vision God has for the church. But how does that desire and change fully penetrate an existing culture? How will the core team know when the change is well grounded and anchored? That will be the focus of the next chapter.

NOTES

1. David Lott, editor, *Conflict Management in Congregations* (Bethesda, Md.: The Alban Institute, 2001) is helpful in understanding conflict and the options available in response to conflict.

2. See *Discerning Your Congregation's Future*, pages 76–84, which offers a plan for "An Evening of Norm Identification."

3. See Alice Mann, *Raising the Roof: The Pastoral-to-Program Size Transition* (Bethesda, Md.: The Alban Institute, 2001).

4. One assessment tool is Christian A. Schwarz, *Natural Church Development* (Carol Stream, Ill.: Church Smart Resources, 1996). *Natural Church Development* identifies "eight essential qualities of healthy churches." A survey is offered that allows a congregation to identify its degree of strength in each of the eight. Repeated use of the survey over a period of time gives the congregation an indication of how effectively it has addressed the needs in an area.

8

Anchoring the Change

Observations from a Mentor

Redevelopment is a journey, and that journey takes you over a lot of territory. At this stage, those who lead the redevelopment process will be different from the people they were at the beginning of the journey. Some new people will be leading but even those not new to the core team will have changed. The church will be different as well and you will want to anchor that difference to ensure that the church does not shift back into what it was several years ago at the beginning of the journey. But anchor what? Preserve what?

Change is not a goal to be reached and then anchored for posterity. Change is a continual process in which you are always moving closer to the expanding vision that God has for you.

Anchoring a Process, Not a Product

Three basic questions have been central to redevelopment: Who are we? Who is our neighbor? Why are we here? At the start of the redevelopment journey the task was to respond to the new, emerging realities in your congregation and community. During the years of the journey these realities change and the church becomes more diverse, reflecting the demographics of the neighborhood. The community itself changes from year to year in its makeup. Perhaps the economic and educational level in the church has shifted. World situations offer new challenges for a faith-filled response.

With those changes, the answers to the three questions also change. The answers at this later point are different from what they were even one year ago, and who you are, who your neighbor is, and why you are here will be different one year from now as well.

What needs to be anchored are the abilities and processes that make it possible for the congregation to respond faithfully to the changes as they are happening. One church started a much-needed well-child clinic to provide immunizations and basic check-ups. Two years later when those services became available through public health services, the church closed the clinic and looked for the next unmet need. Within the year, they started an after-school program for younger children.

Another church developed ways of connecting with a large Hispanic population in the neighborhood. A population shift to predominantly Southeast Asian immigrants called for a change in the focus of the church.

The goal is not simply a transformed church; rather, the goal is a church engaged in the process of continual, ongoing change. And the key to maintaining that ability in the church is individuals remaining open to change in their own lives. Only persons who are giving themselves to continual personal transformation can lead the continual transformation of an institution. If personal transformation stops, church transformation also stops. What will the people in the church do to ensure that they do continue to be in a process of transformation?

How does the core team build processes into the regular life of the church so that the key questions are continually addressed? The demographic makeup of the neighborhood sometimes changes slowly and it often happens without people even being aware of the shift. One church developed a process of doing its own annual demographic study. The church targeted a sample group of blocks for an annual door-to-door census. Basic questions about the major concerns of people give an indication of any shift in needs and values as well as general age, ethnicity, economic demographic, and family life. Using the sample group from year to year gives data about the shifts and gives valuable information about who the neighbors are. With current information about who their neighbor is, a church is receptive to the new vision that God has in mind.

Peak Vitality: Danger and Opportunity

The temptation will be strong to institutionalize the good things that are in place—the structure that works today, the leadership that has come to be trusted, the program and ministries that are strong and satisfying for the people. Things are working well, so why move toward more change? That is all the more reason to take the time and put in the effort.

Every church, every organization has a life cycle from birth to death; however, organizations usually have a great degree of control over the movement along that cycle. Recapturing an inner vitality and an outward focus is almost always possible, but the closer to death the church is when it begins the healing process, the more energy and time it takes.[1] Beginning the process after having started down the slope toward death makes redevelopment hard.

The place in the cycle where it is best to ask the basic identity and mission questions is just before the point of greatest vitality. People are still experiencing energy and new ministries are emerging. Strange as it may seem, that is the best time to engage in a renewal process of moving toward more change. Having reached the point of greatest vitality, people begin quickly to settle in and simply enjoy the achievements. Before long, simple renewal becomes the more involved task of revitalization and finally, if not addressed, the longer and more difficult work of redevelopment.

When you are experiencing vitality is exactly the right time to design ways of again asking basic questions: Who are we? Who is our neighbor? Why are we here? What is the state of the sense of holy urgency in the church? Has the core team continued to evolve so that it has the right makeup for continuing to lead? With the forward movement, is the vision still large enough?

Many churches begin to relax when they are at the point of greatest vitality. Statistics may have shown significant improvement for several years, complacency sets in with confidence that the formula has been found for continued vitality, and the good gains can disappear fast. Healthy, vital churches build in processes that continually open them to new emerging reality. An annual ministry assessment tool indicates specific areas of the church life that need new development.

Storytelling nurtures continual change and continual redevelopment. Stories are told about the challenges and the shifts in the church during the previous years. The adaptive nature of the church is remembered.

One church tells the story of initiating a food bank that combined some basic emergency response services. Inspired by the church, a broader-based, community nonprofit was formed, providing the services in an expanded way. The church, remembering its ability to respond in innovative ways to needs, moved on to a new ministry—an after-school tutoring program accommodating 50 young children from a nearby elementary school. The church continues to initiate ministries in response to needs, letting go of the ministries as needs shift.

The steady flow, the movement forward, is celebrated. Affirming that the church values living out of a sense of holy urgency, the stories also confirm the creativity of the church in responding to whatever emerges. People recall embracing the new opportunities. The stories remind people of their ability to find their way through the challenge of any wilderness.

Empowering Second Generation Leadership

Leading a church into a new place is a challenge, and leading it to that next new place challenges leaders even more. It is important that leaders always be open to the next new place God has in mind; however, what can you reasonably ask of people? Many leaders often stretch themselves far beyond comfort zones as they lead in change. Do they not deserve some stability and time simply to enjoy their accomplishments?

Individuals do have their limits. As part of the process, new leaders need to be recruited and equipped. The new leaders lead to places far beyond even the imaginations of their mentors and coaches. The journey of redevelopment continues as new people are empowered; however, the value of former leaders is not diminished. Their effectiveness is validated as the foundations created by them support new creations. The newly empowered leadership continues to build on the work and the results of their predecessors.

What gets anchored finally is the ability to shift and adapt. Change becomes a normal part of church life and nowhere is that embodied more than in the core team. Their work shapes what becomes the normal and integrated part of the life of the church. They give leadership in discerning the emerging and new ways God calls the church. In order to function in new and creative ways, new members embodying new perspectives and passions join the team. The team is a microcosm of what the church is becoming, continually evolving to reflect the changes in the broader neighborhood. "Who is our neighbor" shifts the makeup of the core team, and the makeup of the core team changes "who we are." "Why we are here" maintains some foundational, essential elements; however, the specifics of the vision shift as "who is our neighbor" and "who we are" changes. The vision and the ways the vision is lived out changes across time. What is anchored is an ongoing process of transformation.

Welcoming and Affirming People

Individuals provide the greatest asset toward an ongoing transformational process. Regarding people as essentially creative, resourceful, and whole provides a welcoming environment. People who can bring change into the organization are affirmed and encouraged to contribute. Welcomed as persons who already have value, new people influence and mold the church and the people in the church. In contrast, people new to the church could be viewed as persons who need to be fixed. Fixing people molds them into images of the persons already present and the church loses the benefit of the gifts brought.

People come to a church with passions and convictions. People come seeking others who feel deeply and who also experience struggles. They seek places where they are welcomed for who they are. They come with an eagerness to give themselves to others and to be part of a creative process. Most want to make a difference in the world.

What will new people experience in your redeveloped church? Will they be invited into servanthood to God and to the world? Or will they be drawn into servitude to an institution?

So much is already present in persons who are creative, resourceful, and whole. The hope for the church and the world is found in God and God is found right there within the people. The call to the church is to help the people discover again what God has planted within them and to encourage them to use their gifts in an outward-focused way.

God has been present in your church since before you began the redevelopment journey, and you passionately want to be used by God in making the difference between life and death for people. With that holy urgency, welcome your neighbor and the gifts from God that they bring. Together with them continue to live into the emerging vision that God has for you and your church.

Reflections of a Companion

I began thinking about leaving the congregation at about the middle of the sixth year. Things were going well at the church and while I knew that our journey of redevelopment was not over, it seemed to be shifting once again. Stability marked this place—and suddenly, everything was easier. New ministries flourished, people felt energized and empowered, our increase in membership continued to reflect the diversity of our community, and even the finances, which the church had struggled with for years, were good.

I attributed my wanderlust to this new phase. I am better at getting things going than I am at finishing them up, I reasoned. Maybe this would be the perfect time to hand the reins over to someone else. The more I thought about it, the more sense it made and the more excited I got. And what excited me? Not the thought of going someplace new, but the idea of leaving. By simply imagining leaving, my breathing slowed and deepened and my body relaxed.

The Ugly Truth

The truth of my desire reached home one Sunday morning during our 11 A.M. contemporary worship service, one of the fruits of our redevelopment. The band, made up mostly of high-school students, played with energy and skill. As I sang, my heart swelled with appreciation for them. And then it hit me. In six months, two of them would depart for college. We would have no keyboard player and no lead guitarist. In a year the other two high-school band members would be preparing to leave. What were we going to do for a band? Without a band what would happen to the contemporary worship service? My thoughts only went downhill from there. What about the youth minister? At some point he would be moving on, which led me to think about our music director. This tremendously gifted musician had settled in our small city as a result of his wife's employment. Her career would inevitably move them again. How could we draw someone of his caliber to our relatively isolated area?

I knew in that moment that it was not boredom that had me contemplating leaving—it was fear. I had provided appropriate leadership up to this point and things were looking great . . . and I wanted to get out of there before it all came crashing down. We had endured so much change—

I was not sure I had the capacity to endure much more. Not only was I tired, but one of my old familiar gremlins had shown up. "You are not really all that competent, you know," he whispered. "You are just lucky. It is simply a matter of time before things start to fall apart. Better get out of here while they still think well of you."

I find the best thing to do with this imaginary creature is to pick him up between my thumb and forefinger, thank him for his concern, and then fling him out of the nearest door or window. Surprisingly, that usually takes care of him. The difficulty comes in recognizing that it is him speaking and not my heart.

Change as a Way of Life

It was absolutely true: the musical leadership of the band would be shifting. It was also true that the whole nature of the contemporary worship service might shift as a result. Might our youth director leave someday? Yep. And it was no secret that our gifted music director, though intensely loyal to our church, longed for the day when his wife's job moved them back to a larger city. People would die; others would be born. Families would move away; new folks would come. Some ministries would end; others would begin. Our neighborhood would continue to shift.

Change was not something we would face just for these years of redevelopment—but always. There was no ending to this journey. The promised land was not a destination we would ever arrive at and live in. It had served and would continue to serve as a compelling vision that would always stay just out of our reach, forcing us to stay adaptive and responsive to the changing times. The changes were not ending, but just beginning. Each year would bring more. My decision to stay or leave might be much more important than I had thought. If I as the leader could not face my anxiety about continual, ongoing change, how could I expect the people to? That day I made the decision to stay and embrace the changes that would continue to come, rather than fight them or run away from them.

The Land of Ongoing and Continuous Change

Once again we faced a critical juncture. Valley View had traveled so far on this journey of redevelopment. They had shaken off their old stiff ways and adapted their behavior and attitudes to meet the needs of the current community. Could they continue adapting as the community continued to change? Had the culture itself changed? A church's culture is formed by the underlying values and norms of the congregation, but to remain vital, the culture of the church needed to have a bias towards ongoing continuous change. At the beginning of the redevelopment process, the culture of Valley View had favored stability over change and tradition over innovation. What about now?

Having arrived in a good place, would the church members say as they had said in the past, "Enough is enough. We're home."—slowly start to congeal again? The current ministries were not what we needed to anchor in our system. Those ministries simply embodied faithful responses to community needs at this point in time. Five years from now, the community might have very different needs and thus require different ministry responses. Anchoring ministries in our system might eventually lead us to the same mired place where we had started and require a whole new round of change. An adaptive flexible culture was what needed anchoring. So what we practiced was flexing and shifting.

Passing the reigns became the hallmark of this period in our church's life. Team leaders were encouraged to be on the lookout for people with leadership potential. The church council and I charged ourselves with the task of developing a new generation of leaders. Storytelling, which had been an important part of early phases of redevelopment, proved to be helpful in this task too. We learned once again that stories could carry many meanings depending on how they were told.

For instance, the story of the after-school program could be told to point out a new and well-running ministry. This interpretation reinforced the notion, however, that we had arrived at the promised land and that leaders did their job when they too developed successful programs. That was not the lesson to be learned, so we did not want to tell stories from a perspective that would imply that. The same story could also be told to illustrate the new culture we valued: how a small group of people linked their deep passions to address the community's great need. When stories highlighted the shifts in form the program took over the years, those stories said we valued discernment and adaptive behavior. Stories told from that perspective helped our emerging leaders understand the culture and the task we were asking them to undertake.

We had learned that we as a church could move from point A to point B; however, the question remained as to whether we could then move from point B to point C.

An Adaptive and Flexible Culture

We were forced to address the issue of flexibility when some of our "original" new ministries were called to adapt. Only three years old, the bilingual playgroup faced that challenge first. Created as a venue for Spanish- and English-speaking children to develop friendships and appreciation for each other's culture, the group became aware of the city's small Korean population. The playgroup was thriving just as it was; in fact, more children would make the current space unusable. Parents liked things as they were. "If it's not broken, don't fix it," people said.

As the leadership reflected further, however, the original intent was not only to provide a multicultural experience for children, but to plant seeds of understanding and cooperation that might result in better ethnic relations in our community when the children grew up. With that in mind, the benefits of including the Korean children far outweighed the costs. The group reconfigured itself and continued to thrive, although very differently. That story spoke powerfully to our congregation about our ability to adapt.

As other groups successfully navigated second-generation changes and thrived, we came to believe that ongoing transformation was not only possible, it was what we wanted. A second generation of leaders took over. A look around the core team one evening revealed a crew of people that included none of the original core team members. Many of them had not attended Valley View when the original core team was formed. Most of the original core team members were still active in the church and highly supportive, but they had passed the reins, making room for new people and new ideas.

Am I ready to leave now? Yes and no. There is no other church I would rather serve. There are no other people with whom I would rather journey. I do not want to leave. Yet I have been feeling that inner tug, which says that something else is calling me. And so it starts.

What is it like for your congregation as you work through this step of the redevelopment process? I would be curious to hear what you miss about the old ways and what you love about the new. After their long wilderness journey, the Israelites had mixed feelings about finally entering the promised land. As they drew close, they sent out scouts to see what this long-awaited land was like. Some returned with tales of a land that flowed with milk and honey. Others reported that the land was full of terrible giants. Conflicting perceptions are normal, even as a church prepares to take its final steps. Blessings as you work with the coach to take the final step.

Guidance from a Coach

At this eighth step in the redevelopment process, the core team finds itself at a crossroads. It is time to decide if you really want to anchor the capacity for change in the culture of this church. If so, this will mean that redevelopment will become the norm for your church, to always be looking for the new directions in which God is leading it. Therefore, change will become the standard way of being.

To achieve this kind of inherent adaptability, the core team wants to make sure that the abilities and processes that make it possible to respond to God's expanding vision are well anchored. As the mentor and companion sections have pointed out through counsel and stories, this anchoring is done by revisiting the previous steps in the redevelopment process and constantly giving fresh attention to them. This becomes the never-ending journey of redevelopment, allowing us to be faithful and intentional about living out God's intent for the church and for individuals within the church.

Reflect and Journal

The goal for this coaching section is for the core team to develop a plan for anchoring the capacity for change in the culture of the church. In preparing to address this goal, consider the extent to which the process of redevelopment is presently anchored in your church. Record your assessment of the following areas with as much detail as possible in your journal.

- To what degree are you individually, and the core team as a group, demonstrating a value in personal spiritual growth and transformation? What have you read lately? What have you studied lately? Have you spent time apart lately? Where do you spend time in service? What has prayer revealed to you recently?

- What are the nature, frequency, and accessibility of the spiritual growth and transformational opportunities available to the congregation? What percentage of the congregation participates?

- Review the ways in which the core team continues to listen for the sense of holy urgency that God has planted in the people of your church.

- Review the ways the core team continues to listen for, and share about the evolving vision of the church. Are the three basic questions of "Who are we? Who is our neighbor? Why are we here?" still being asked and re-asked? Is the behavior of the core team consistent with what the core team says and writes about the vision? How might you confirm this?

- Consider the ways that people are empowered for ministry in the church. Look for evidence that a broadening base of people is constantly being empowered and equipped for ministry and leadership.

- Have you been willing to address the barriers that have limited people's ability to respond to God's vision? In what ways? What barriers currently exist?

- What methods are you using to continue to celebrate ways in which the vision is being lived into? How are you lifting up the results of living in a different way? How are those stories being shared? Is a variety of feedback being provided by a variety of people, or does it appear as if only one or two people are convinced of the value of living into the vision?

- How do you go about identifying who future leaders will be? As a current leader, what is going on in your heart and your head as you consider the question of future leaders?

- List other things to clarify the present degree to which the capacity for change is anchored in the culture of the church.

Develop a Plan

Next, review the following suggested plan to achieve your goal of anchoring the capacity for change in the culture of the church.

- Identify ways that the core team can be even more explicit in demonstrating its commitment to personal spiritual growth and transformation. For example, is it common knowledge that all members of the core team participate in weekly Bible studies? Or has the core team recently spent a weekend away together in prayer and reflection?

- If the present condition indicates a need here, develop a plan to broaden the short-term and long-term spiritual growth opportunities for your congregation and beyond. Include a time line for implementation and a plan for evaluation of effectiveness.

- Determine ways to strengthen your system of listening for the sense of holy urgency that God has planted in the people of your church. Review the suggested procedures outlined in chapter 1. Are there additional ways you need to listen, such as focused conversations with each group of new members around the time they join the church?

- Determine strategies to strengthen your system to listen for the evolving vision for the church. Review the suggested procedures in chapter 3 and determine the steps needed in your setting. Do you have a plan to annually review the nature and makeup of your surrounding community? As you listen to current perceptions and understandings about the holy urgency and God's vision for the church, are there shifts to be made in the church's vision?

- Identify more opportunities for people to own and be owned by the vision. Review the suggested procedures in chapter 4, watching for underutilized ways to communicate about the vision. For example, one church realized that while they did a good job of responding to the needs in the community surrounding the church, they rarely mentioned that it flowed out of their understanding of God's vision for the church. As a result, they set up a system of monthly sharing in worship. Examples included biweekly newsletters and Web site articles in which individuals shared their experiences of personal transformation through this service, and how they saw these experiences as part of living out God's vision for the church.

- Develop a plan in which more people can be empowered to respond to their understanding of God's vision for them. Review the suggested procedures in chapter 5, giving careful consideration to helping people discover their gifts and passions. Assess how you provide needed skill training and mentor new leaders. Consider the effectiveness of these systems in empowering people.

- Given your assessment of what barriers currently exist, develop an updated plan to address each barrier. Review the recommended processes for dealing with barriers in chapter 5. The core team will want to confer with involved people outside the core team to assess the effectiveness of the updated plan.

- Determine ways to strengthen your system of celebrating the vision being realized in your church. Review the recommended procedures in chapter 6 to better utilize the stories of the people. Consider how people experience the results and benefits of living in a different way, with a focus now on God's vision for the church.

- Determine ways to identify future leaders, people who value living into God's vision for the church. Include a plan for bringing new people onto the core team.

- List other options you have identified to achieve your goal.

Chart a Course

Next, consider the suggested plan above for achieving your goal. Determine what steps you will take to anchor the capacity for change in the culture of your church. Develop the specific plans you will need to implement them. Consider what it will take for you and the core team to be accountable to your plans. How will you ensure this?

NOTES

    1.   See the life-cycle chart in the preface.

Overwhelmed by the prospect of entering an eight-stage process that will take years to become a way of life? Daunted by the time, energy, and focus redevelopment demands? Take a deep breath and relax. Every long journey is really just a series of tiny steps—days lived one by one. Be attentive to how you live your days. The weeks and years will take care of themselves.

As you work with an overarching process of change in your church, you yourself will be changing. The big changes in the system will happen only as the little ones occur in individuals. The small changes that happen in you each day are the seeds for the changes that will take place in the larger church.

Do Not Bring a Plan into the World—Bring Yourself

The most important thing you can bring to this journey is yourself. Begin your day with a time of centering that reminds you who you are and whose you are. Then, let the activities of that day flow from a sense of deep integrity. Allow what is within you, your best gifts and your deepest hopes, to interact with what is out there in the world. Let your energy and focus flow to where God would have it go. At night, look back on the day and hallow it as one that God made and was present in. As the day ends give thanks for it and declare it done. Begin fresh when you wake the next morning.

Questions for Each Day

• As you start the day, how will you show up? What attitude will dominate in you throughout the day? What aspect of God will you reflect?

• As you move through the day, what will you do? Why? For what purpose?

• As you finish the day, what meaning do you assign to it? Where was God in this day?

Consider these questions each day for a week and you will be changed. You will notice more how you spend your time and your energy and the meaning you assign to the things that happen to you. The ways in which you live your life will become more of a conscious choice.

Do this each day for a year and the groups you are a part of will be different. You cannot change without the groups you are a part of changing.

Do this each day for seven years and your church will be different, for the groups cannot change without the church changing.

Be intentional about who you are and what you do. Your conscious awareness of God's presence in the midst of your days will influence you and the choices you make. Through those simple daily choices, God will transform you and through you transform your church.

You do not bring a plan into the world—you bring yourself. It is in the interaction between you, the world, and God that the plan emerges. Leave behind your preconceived notions. The most important thing you bring to the journey is yourself—and God is with you. Let the plan unfold.

So breathe. God wants nothing more than for you and your faith community to be an outpost of God's love and justice. Open yourself to the people around you and to your essential self, and let God work. Amen.

Blanchard, Kenneth, Drea Zigarmi, and Patricia Zigarmi. *Leadership and the One-Minute Manager.* New York: William Morrow & Company, 1985.

Bridges, William. *Managing Transitions.* Reading, Mass.: Addison-Wesley Publishing Company, 1991.

Buckingham, Marcus, and Donald O. Clifton. *Now Discover Your Strengths.* New York: The Free Press, 2001.

Edwards, Tilden. *Living in the Presence: Spiritual Exercises to Open Our Lives to the Awareness of God.* San Francisco: HarperSanFrancisco, 1995.

Gaede, Beth, editor. *Size Transitions.* Bethesda, Md.: The Alban Institute, 2001.

Kotter, John P. *Leading Change.* Boston: Harvard Business School Press, 1996.

Lott, David, editor. *Conflict Management in Congregations.* Bethesda, Md.: The Alban Institute, 2001.

Mann, Alice. *Can Our Church Live? Redeveloping Congregations in Decline.* Bethesda, Md.: The Alban Institute, 1999.

Mann, Alice. *Raising the Roof: The Pastoral-to-Program Size Transition.* Bethesda:, Md. The Alban Institute, 2001.

Mann, Alice. *The In Between Church.* Bethesda, Md.: The Alban Institute, 1998.

Morseth, Ellen. *Ritual and the Arts in Spiritual Discernment.* Kansas City, Mo.: Worshipful-Work, 1999.

Oswald, Roy M., and Robert E. Friedrich, Jr. *Discerning Your Congregation's Future: A Strategic and Spiritual Approach.* Bethesda, Md.: The Alban Institute, 1996.

Owen, Harrison. *The Spirit of Leadership*. San Francisco: Berret-Koehler Publications, 1999.

Quinn, Robert E. *Change the World*. San Francisco: Jossey-Bass Publishers, 2000.

Quinn, Robert E. *Deep Change*. San Francisco: Jossey-Bass Publishers, 1996.

Rendle, Gilbert R. *Leading Change in the Congregation*. Bethesda, Md.: The Alban Institute, 1998.

Schwartz, Christian A. *Natural Church Development*. Carol Stream, Ill.: Church Smart Resources, 1996.

Schwartz, Christian A. *The Three Colors of Ministry: A Trinitarian Approach to Identifying and Developing Your Spiritual Gifts*. St. Charles, Ill.: Church Smart Resources, 2001.

Thompson, Marjorie J. *Soul Feast: An Invitation to the Christian Spiritual Life*. Louisville, Ky.: Westminister John Knox Press, 1995.

Wilber, Ken. *A Theory of Everything*. Boston: Shambhala, 2000.

Wills, Dick. *Waking to God's Dream*. Nashville: Abingdon Press, 1999.

Welcome to the work of Alban Institute...
the leading publisher and congregational resource organization for clergy and laity today.

Your purchase of this book means you have an interest in the kinds of information, research, consulting, networking opportunities and educational seminars that Alban Institute produces and provides. We are a non-denominational, non-profit 25-year-old membership organization dedicated to providing practical and useful support to religious congregations and those who participate in and lead them.

Alban is acknowledged as a pioneer in learning and teaching on *Conflict Management *Faith and Money *Congregational Growth and Change *Leadership Development *Mission and Planning *Clergy Recruitment and Training *Clergy Support, Self-Care and Transition *Spirituality and Faith Development *Congregational Security.

Our membership is comprised of over 8,000 clergy, lay leaders, congregations and institutions who benefit from:
❖ 15% discount on hundreds of Alban books
❖ $50 per-course tuition discount on education seminars
❖ Subscription to *Congregations*, the Alban journal (a $30 value)
❖ Access to Alban research and (soon) the "Members-Only" archival section of our web site www.alban.org

For more information on Alban membership or to be added to our catalog mailing list, call 1-800-486-1318, ext.243 or return this form.

Name and Title: _____

Congregation/Organization: _____

Address: _____

City: _____ Tel.: _____

State: _____ Zip: _____ Email: _____

BKIN

The Alban Institute
Attn: Membership Dept.
7315 Wisconsin Avenue
Suite 1250 West
Bethesda, MD 20814-3211